How to Write Your Own Will

2nd Edition

How to Write Your Own Will

2nd Edition

John C. Howell

LIBERTY HOUSE®

SECOND EDITION
FIRST PRINTING

Copyright © 1989, 1985 by John C. Howell
Reproduction or publication of the content in any manner, without express permission of the publisher, is prohibited. The publisher takes no responsibility for the use of any of the materials or methods described in this book, or for the products thereof. Printed in the United States of America, LIBERTY HOUSE books are published by LIBERTY HOUSE, a division of TAB BOOKS Inc. Its trademark, consisting of the words "LIBERTY HOUSE" and the portrayal of Benjamin Franklin, is registered in the United States Patent and Copyright Office.

Published by:
   LIBERTY HOUSE
   A Division of
   TAB BOOKS Inc.
   Blue Ridge Summit, PA 17294

Library of Congress Cataloging in Publication Data

Howell, John Cotton, 1926-
      How to write your own will/ by John C. Howell. —2nd ed.
         p.   cm.
      Includes index.
      ISBN 0-8306-0352-2 (pbk.)
      1. Wills—United States—Popular works. 2. Holographic wills-
   -United States—Popular works. 3. Wills—United States—Forms.
   I. Title.
KF755.Z9HZ   1989
346.7305′4—dc   89-2323
[347.30654]   CIP

TAB BOOKS Inc. offers software for sale. For information and a catalog, please contact TAB Software Department, Blue Ridge Summit, PA 17294-0850.

Questions regarding the content of this book should be addressed to:

      Reader Inquiry Branch
      Editorial Department
      TAB BOOKS Inc.
      Blue Ridge Summit, PA 17294

Acquisitions Editor: Kimberly Tabor
Book Editor: Gileen P. Baylus

Contents

Form and Certainty of Instrument • Rules of Construction •
Acknowledgment and Recording of Documents •
Duration and Revocation of Power of Attorney •
Consent of Spouse • The Durable Power of Attorney •
Statutory Provisions • How to Complete Your Power of Attorney

Preface

A majority of the people in America—estimated at 87½ percent—do not have a current, valid will. Many people do not know the meaning or significance of *avoiding probate*, and don't fully understand how a simple living trust can save thousands of dollars in probate costs. Some people are not sure what the terms *probate* and *probate proceedings* mean, and might not know the difference between a Last Will and Testament and a Living Will. How do you make a Power of Attorney into a Durable Power of Attorney? What is a *durable* power? Can you prepare any of these without a lawyer? Should you?

The purpose of this book is to explain these estate planning terms, explain estate planning, discuss the significance of the various methods and techniques for planning your own estate, and explore the potential for you to do your own estate planning, or some of it, in appropriate circumstances. Whether you do it yourself or employ professionals, the information in this book will be helpful.

You can prepare your own will in the privacy of your own home without a lawyer. You can explore the advisability of avoiding probate with respect to some, or all, of your assets—depending upon the facts and circumstances, and in appropriate circumstances, you can do it yourself. You can learn how to handle many aspects of probate proceedings, and how to assist your attorney in the administration of an estate—all of which is designed to save you and the estate a lot of money.

During the past few years medical science has developed the technology to sustain and prolong life almost indefinitely. This has generated a national debate about patients who suffer from a terminal condition in which there is a reasonable degree of medical certainty that there can be no recovery and the patient's death is imminent. Many of these patients are incompetent or incapacitated to the extent that they lack sufficient understanding or capacity to make or communicate responsible decisions regarding medical treatment. The Durable Power of Attorney and Living Will, now authorized in most states by recent statutory enactments, are estate planning tools designed to ameliorate the anxiety of those who claim such life prolonging techniques are an intrusive threat to their right to die a peaceful, dignified, and natural death.

This book will help you with legal matters that you can handle yourself, and help you effectively communicate with your lawyer in those cases where you need a lawyer. If you encounter difficulties or uncertainty—or just want to—it is appropriate to consult with competent professionals. Because statutes and court decisions vary by states and are subject to modification, no liability is assumed by the author or publisher regarding the use of this book.

Be wise today;
'tis madness to defer.

Edward Young (1683-1765)

Part 1
How to Write
Your Own Will

Chapter 1

What Is a Will?

Estate planning is the process of planning the creation, accumulation, conservation, and utilization of estate resources to secure the maximum benefit now, during life, during disability, during retirement, and after death.

Your will is one of the more important parts of a good estate plan, second in importance only to avoiding probate. All property owned by a decedent must be transferred to others in a legal way either by gift, will, by operation of law, living trust, or other probate and estate planning methods, or by a combination of these techniques.

You can write your own legal will without a lawyer, in the privacy of your own home. You will need complete information and instructions about the will writing process, the essential elements of a will, the laws governing wills, and the necessary forms for use in writing a will. This book is designed to provide all of the information and help you need to accomplish most of your estate planning objectives.

You can use this information for all adult members of your family. If you can overcome the inhibitions of talking about estate planning, this can be an interesting and worthwhile family project. Estate planning is an extremely important subject to all members of your family. Your will is effective only for transfer of those assets in your estate at the time of death. Assets transferred outside of the probate system by joint ownership with right of survivorship, living trusts, gifts, or other probate avoidance techniques would not be affected by your will. Avoiding federal estate taxes was once a major consideration in estate planning; however, under current federal tax laws there is an unlimited marital deduction (no tax on assets left to a spouse) and each estate has a $600,000 exemption.

Another advantage of using this book is that you can change your estate plans at any time you have a need for change—or if you simply change your mind. Many people like to have this flexibility in their estate planning.

Writing your own will is now as simple and easy as writing a letter.

Definitions

A *will* is an instrument executed by a competent person in the manner prescribed by statute, whereby he makes a disposition of his property to take effect on and after his death. A document, to be a will, must be testamentary in character, and must be executed in accordance with the requirements of the applicable state statute. An instrument is testamentary in character if, from the language used, it is apparent that the writer intended to make a disposition of his property, or some part of it, to be effective at death. In the absence of testamentary intent (*animus testandi*), there is no will. It is, of course, essential that a testator know and understand the contents of his will. A disposition of property is not a necessary requirement of a will even though it is generally the main reason most people write a will. A person can make a will for the sole purpose of nominating an executor or appointing a guardian.

A will must be *ambulatory*, that is, subject to change, and revocable during the maker's lifetime. The Latin phrase, *ambulatoria voluntas*, a changeable will, denotes the power that a testator possesses of altering his will during his lifetime. The term *testament*, in early common-law days, referred only to a disposition of real property. In modern use, the term *will* includes every kind of testamentary act taking effect from the mind of the testator and manifested by an instrument in writing executed and attested in accordance with the statutes. Any writing, however informal it might be, made with the intent to dispose of property at the death of the writer, if executed in accordance with the statutory requirements, might be a good testamentary disposition. A letter, postcard, memo, informal notes on envelopes, and other informal writings might constitute a will if they have the essential elements of a will. Also, it is not essential in all states to have a will witnessed if certain other requirements are met.

For example, a *nuncupative will* is one that is not in writing, and exists only when the testator declares his will orally before witnesses. A *holographic will* or *olographic* will, valid in 23 states, is one that is entirely written and signed (and in some states, dated) by the testator in his own handwriting.

A *codicil* is some addition to, qualification of, or change of, one's will. A *bequest* is a gift of personal property, while a *legacy* is a gift of property under a will. *Devise* means a gift of real property by will. A *devisor* is the one who leaves real property, while the *devisee* is the one who inherits real property through a devise.

An *acknowledgment* is a formal declaration before an authorized official, by a person who executed an instrument, that it is his free act and deed. If the decedent leaves a will designating a personal representative, the proper title for that representative is *executor* or *executrix*. (Throughout the rest of this book, the male-gender term *executor* will be used for both executor and executrix.) A *guardian* is a person lawfully vested with the power, and charged with the duty of taking care of a person and managing the property rights of another person, who, for some peculiarity of status or defect of age, understanding, or self-control, is considered incapable of administering his own affairs.

Intestate is the status of one who dies without a will. A *testator* (male) or *testatrix* (female) is one who dies leaving a will. The words *execution, subscribe,* and *subscription* simply refer to signing an instrument, usually at the end of it. In some states it is an absolute statutory requirement that a will be signed at the end. Attestation consists in witnessing the execution of the will by the testator in order to see and take notes mentally that those things are done that the statute requires for the execution of a will, and that the signature of the testator exists as a fact. The primary purpose of requiring that a will be attested is to render available proof that there has been a compliance with the statutory requisites of the execution of a will, and that the instrument offered for probate is the exact paper that the alleged testator signed, and not a surreptitious will, fraudulently substituted. Publication of a will consists in the communication by the testator to the attesting witnesses at the time they attest the instrument of his intention that it shall take effect as his will.

The Nature of Wills

To determine whether or not an instrument is a will, your intentions while writing the will must be ascertained. If you intend to dispose of your estate, the instrument is generally considered testamentary in character. The testamentary character of an instrument is determined by the interpretation of, and from the construction of, the language you use when writing the instrument. If it is clear that your intention is to dispose of your property after your death, the document contains sufficient testamentary character to constitute a will. The courts, in the interpretation of a will, generally consider the instrument as a whole. What property you have and how you intend to dispose of it must be clearly stated in the will. This cannot be done for you after your demise. The *intent* refers to an intent to dispose of property, not an intent to make a will. In other words, unless there is an intention to dispose of property, there is no will.

Predicatory Words

Unfortunately many people state in wills that they "wish" or "hope" or "desire" that certain things will occur with respect to their property. These words, when used in a will merely to suggest that the property be disposed of in a certain way are not generally legally binding. Words that do not clearly indicate an intent to specifically dispose of your property should not be used. It is critical to avoid such terminology altogether or at least state as clearly as possible in writing what your true intentions are. The use of unclear language is an open invitation to lawsuits.

It is also essential that you know the contents of your will. It is usually presumed that a person who signs a written instrument knows the contents thereof, but this can be questioned. Uncertainty regarding these issues can be avoided by following the checklist presented later in this book. A will written in a language that you do not understand still might be effective if you know and understand the contents. In fact, a blind person can validly sign a will if he knows and understands the contents of that will and has an intent to dispose of property.

Contents of Wills

There is no magic formula for what should be in a will, but the usual items include the following:

- a statement identifying the testator
- special instructions on payment of debts
- burial instructions and other general matters
- appointment of executor or executrix, trustee, or guardian
- general and special disposition of property
- residuary clause
- execution and attestation

Never place scandalous or derogatory matters in a will because this is another open invitation to unnecessary litigation. If scandalous matter does appear in a will, the court will usually disregard it; it has no place and it serves no purpose whatsoever. A properly executed will, under most laws, must be admitted to probate when offered.

Uncertain Provisions of Wills

The language you use in a will should be easily understood. When in doubt, it is better to use your own choice of words rather than to try to make the will sound "legal." It is necessary for a will to have a definite subject, in terms of property, and a definite or ascertainable object, in terms of persons, in order for there to be a valid disposition of property. Most courts will make an effort to correctly determine and interpret from the will just what you want so that your intentions can be carried out. This, indeed, is a major objective of the laws governing wills. A will that makes no disposition of property, but gives the executor "full authority" to divide the estate is void. It simply is not a will as

defined by law in terms of accomplishing your objectives. You cannot let someone else do it for you, but you can establish a trust, appoint a trustee, and grant
powers of appointment.

Alterations and Changes

Writing between the lines and using erasures in a will are not recommended;
if changes are desirable, retype the will. However, if changes are made in
accordance with the formalities required by law, the will as changed and altered
probably will be admitted to probate. Any changes made in the will after your
death can form no part of the will, and are of no effect whatsoever. Any changes
in a will made by someone other than the testator himself and without his knowledge or consent, or with a bad motive or intention to deceive, or by accident
or mistake, will not be effective. You can change your will as often as you choose,
but it must be done strictly in accordance with the mandatory requirements of
law.

Fraud, Mistake, and Undue Influence

Fraud, mistake, or undue influence are reasons for contesting the probate
of a will or setting aside the probate of a will. The terms *fraud* and *undue
influence* are closely associated and frequently are used together in most
situations involving the contest of a will. The words *fraud, duress,* and *undue
influence* frequently are used interchangeably by most courts. Some merely
adopt the use of one word or the other depending upon the facts of the case.
Using a broad generalization, undue influence is a type of fraud, even though
it might have taken place without an active, affirmative, false statement or evil,
wicked, and corrupt motive. Some courts have stated that a fraudulent intent
or motive is essential to cause undue influence to the point of invalidating a will.
Other courts have stated that any influence that might have persuaded you when
you wrote the will does not necessarily have to be fraudulent in order to invalidate
the will. This is another legal issue that has no easy answer. Undue influence
might be fraudulently exerted, but it is not inseparably connected with fraud.
On the other hand, fraud might constitute a ground for contesting the validity
of a will independent of undue influence. In all events the courts frequently
struggle with a precise definition of the terms, but when a decision is made,
it is usually a judgment based upon all the facts and circumstances. The courts
merely use the appropriate words, phrases, or terms to state the conclusion
reached.

If it can be established by good evidence that your will was written in error,
the will might be declared void. In the absence of a law to the contrary, the
validity of a will is not affected by a mistake of law unless fraud or undue influence
was forced upon you or the mistake involves a want of testamentary intent.

An example is one where you might execute the wrong instrument. The word *mistake* is used here in the sense of describing a chain of events or circumstances around which you sign the will, but because of the chain of events you did not intend to execute a valid will. A will is usually not denied probate merely because you do not understand or appreciate the effect of language used, so long as you have an intent to make a will.

Some laws provide that a *mistake of fact* can nullify in part the operation of a will provided that such a mistake is the result of ignorance and not an error of judgment after investigation or willful failure to make a proper investigation when the truth could have been determined. As a general rule, the courts will not declare an entire will invalid because of a *mistake* as to one phrase or paragraph.

Sufficient undue influence that might invalidate a will is not easy to define. Undue influence refers to the means and methods used by a person for the purpose of affecting and overcoming another. Undue influence is that which substitutes the wishes of another for your own wishes. It has often been stated that undue influence is an *unlawful influence*. It appears, however, that nothing more is meant by the expression than that it is the influence that deprives you of your freedom to act as you wish. A will can be contested successfully because of undue influence even though none of the acts that caused the influence might result in a civil or criminal liability charge. Acts performed with a good motive can nevertheless constitute undue influence.

The legal issues generated by claims of fraud, mistakes, or undue influence are very difficult to resolve. A careful review of this book, an analysis of your estate, and a properly drafted will can avoid all of these potential problems. Extra effort in the preparation and execution of your will can avoid the necessity of having some member of your family presented with these difficult questions in the future.

What Is Meant by a Basic Will or a Simple Will?

As a general rule, a one or two page will is entirely adequate for most people, married or unmarried. The term *simple will* is broadly and generally used in legal circles to describe a will for any person who does not have significant estate tax problems or legal entanglements requiring special provisions. Under the new tax code, estate taxes generally do not become a problem until the taxable estate exceeds $600,000, (the exempt amount after 1986) and, of course, there is an unlimited marital exemption. Lawyers are sometimes reluctant to refer to a client's will as simple because they don't want the client to think his estate is small, and might not want the client to get the impression that the client's will is easy to prepare. In this book, the term *basic will* is used to describe the great majority of wills for estates with no significant estate tax problems and no unusual legal entanglements. This covers the vast majority of Americans.

Essentially, in the absence of major tax or legal problems, the purpose of a will is rather basic: one simply appoints a representative and makes a disposition of property.

The basic will avoids the inconvenience and uncertainty of intestacy—the status of dying without any will. At the same time, you can appoint your executor or guardian to handle the administration of the estate rather than having some probate judge appoint one. Moreover, you can minimize the expenses of administration by waiving bonds in appropriate circumstances. If you fail to appoint an executor or guardian, there will be legal fees incurred in the proceedings to have the probate court make appointments. In most cases, it also causes some delays. Most married persons, with or without children, generally wish to have the entire estate go to the surviving spouse. This might not happen if you do not have a will. The basic will also makes provision for appointment of a guardian for minor children in the event of simultaneous deaths or where a spouse is predeceased, and a provision for a trust for minors.

Thus, the basic will is all that is needed by most people. The basic will for an unmarried person is essentially the same as the basic will for married persons, with minor changes to delete certain provisions, such as common disaster clauses. Marital deduction clauses are no longer needed because there is now an unlimited marital exemption.

Chapter 2

Special Kinds of Wills

While the primary purpose of this book is to enable you to understand the basic legal principles governing wills, enable you to draft your own will, and execute your will in accordance with the statutory requirements of your state, there are some special kinds of wills with which you should become familiar. These include the holographic (handwritten) will and the nuncupative (oral) will. There are also special wills under the Louisiana Civil Code, but these aren't discussed, since the holographic will might be the best method for residents of that state.

Holographic Wills

Some state statutes permit a person to write a valid holographic will in his own handwriting with no witnesses needed, while others do not. Some of the statutes require that the will be written, dated, and signed entirely in the testator's own handwriting. Other statutes, based on the Uniform Probate Code, require only that the signature and the material provisions of the will be in the testator's handwriting. By requiring only the material provisions to be in the testator's handwriting, such holographic wills might be valid even though immaterial parts, such as the date or introductory wording, be printed or stamped. Under these statutes a valid holographic will might even be executed on some printed forms if the printed portion could be eliminated and the handwritten portion could evidence the testator's will. For some persons unable to obtain legal assistance, the holographic will is entirely adequate.

A holographic will is an unwitnessed, unattested will that is entirely in the testator's handwriting. The holographic will as a distinct type originated in French law. Express provision for it was made in the Code of Napoleon; and this provision, in substantially the same form, was carried over into the Louisiana Civil Code. According to Section 970 of the Code Napoleon,

"A holographic testament shall not be valid, unless it be written entirely, dated and signed by the testator with his own hand; it is subject to no other form."

The recognition given such an instrument as a valid testamentary instrument despite the lack of compliance with the formalities of attestation is attributed to the fact that a successful counterfeit of another's handwriting is exceedingly difficult and that the requirement that it be in the testator's handwriting would afford protection against forgery. Although written by the testator himself, a holographic will is a solemn act; and no matter how clearly it conveys the wishes of the decedent, if it does not meet the statutory requirements, it is not valid. It is sufficient if the writing expresses, however informally, a testamentary purpose in language sufficiently clear to be understood.

A Letter as a Holographic Will

Because a holographic will is one that is entirely written and signed by the testator in his own handwriting, a letter in the handwriting of the testator might qualify as a will although it is not witnessed if it has the necessary testamentary character. A simple letter is the most common type of instrument sought to be probated as a will or codicil. Many people prefer the holographic method of disposing of their property.

In authorizing letters testamentary in character to be admitted to probate, the courts have attached no particular significance to the type of letter involved. Even a postcard can be probated as a will or codicil provided it is testamentary in character and meets the requisites of a handwritten will. Even if a letter does not meet the formal requisites of a will or codicil in the state where it is sought to be probated, if it meets the requisites in the state where it was written, it might, under applicable statutes, be probated as a valid will.

In order to be a will, it is an absolute requirement that the document be signed by the testator. This does not always mean a legal or formal signature. Any form of signature, even though it is abbreviated, will be approved if it is possible to identify the signer as the person involved. If the document was signed with an intent to dispose of property, it is generally held to be a valid will.

Some state statutes require that a holographic will be dated, as well as signed and written, in the hand of the testator. Under statutes requiring a date, the year, month, and day must be given, according to most courts. The fact that the letter is dated incorrectly does not render it void.

A letter dictated by the writer and actually written by a third person, or typewritten, either by the decedent or by someone on his behalf, or printed, does not meet the requisites of a holographic will, and is governed by the ordinary rules applicable to formal wills. This means that such a document would require signing and witnessing as in the case of regular statutory wills.

Testamentary Character

In order for a document, such as a letter, to be a last will and testament, it must, in addition to meeting all other legal requirements, clearly show that the decedent intended it to take effect only after his death. It is also necessary that it appear from the document that the decedent intended, by the very paper itself, to make a disposition of his property after his death. Testamentary character of the document is not the testator's realization that it is a will, but his intention to create a revocable disposition of his property. Casual statements, suggestions, wishes, recommendations, or requests are not dispositive, and generally do not make a will.

By way of example, the following writings have been held by the courts to be of sufficient testamentary intent to make a valid holographic will.

- "This is to serifey that ie levet to mey wife Real and persnal and she to dispose for them as she wis . . ." (dated and signed, is not vague and uncertain, and devises to the wife all the real and personal property of the husband). *Mitchell, et al., v. Donahue, 34 P 614 (Calif 1893).*
- "dear bill i want you to have farm Annie Kaufman." *In re Kaufman's Will, 365 Pa 555, 76 A 414.*
- "Dear old Nance: I wish to give you my watch, two shawls, and also five thousand dollars. Your old friend, E. A. Gordon." *Clarke v. Ransom, 50 Cal 595.*
- "If I die or get killed in Texas, the place must belong to you, and I would not want you to sell it." *Alston v. Davis, 118 N.C. 202, 24 S.E. 15.*
- "July 7, 1949
  "Dear Catherine:
     "Just a few lines to let you know I am starting to Monaco, and I was very pleased with the vacation. Catherine, I want you to know you are to get all I have when I die. Tell Mary Agnes and David that Uncle George said hello and give them a big hug and kiss for me.
     "I remain as ever
        "Uncle George Thompson." *Appeal of James Thompson, 375 Pa 193, 100 A 2d 69, 40 A.L.R. 2d 694.*
- ". . . if enny thing happens all . . . (money bonds, saving stamps and home) goes to George Darl & Irvin Kepp this letter lock it up it may help you out." *Re Kimmel's Estate, 278 Pa 435, 123 A 405.*

On the other hand, a statement in a letter that "After all is said and done I intend to leave you and Reba what I have some day," did not show testamentary intent. *Poff v. Kaufman, 276 S.W. 2d 432.*

Signature

The important factor in determining whether the signature on a letter offered as a will or codicil is sufficient though abbreviated or otherwise different from the formal signature of the writer is whether the word or words were affixed to the paper with the intent that they constitute a signature, and sufficiently show who signed the paper.

As a general rule, the courts have held that the signing of a descriptive title relating to relationships, such as mother, father, brother, or aunt, is valid as a signature to a holographic will if the testator or testatrix wrote with the intent to execute the will. The courts have generally held that initials are sufficient if signed with the intent to execute the holographic will.

For example, the following have been held as valid signatures:

- "Your loving mother."
- "Father" *Re Kimmel's Estate (1924) 278 Pa 435, 123 A 405.*
- "Pop" *Kling, Sr. Estate (1956) 12 Pa D & C 2d 588.*
- "Brother Alex" *Wise v. Short (1921) 181 N.C. 320, 197 S.E. 134.*
- "Ant Nanie" *Wells v. Lewis (1921) 190 Ky 626, 228 S.W. 3.*
- "Lus" *Cartwright v. Cartwright, (1923) 158 Ark 278, 250 S.W. 11.*

Date

A date has been held not essential to the validity of a holographic will unless it is expressly required by statute. Where the date is required by statute, as in some states, it must be dated by the testator in his own handwriting. The date adds verity to the instrument; if the instrument is a forgery the date might furnish the means of detecting the fraud. The date might also be important in some cases to determine the testamentary capacity of the testator. Moreover, if there are two or more wills it is essential to have dates to determine the priorities of the documents. In those states where a date is required the courts have been strict in requiring that the date be definite, complete, and certain. Usually the day, month, and year are required.

Holographic Wills under the Uniform Probate Code

The Uniform Code recommends the authorization of holographic wills and suggests more liberal wording in the statutes. The recommended language of the Uniform Code for the holographic will statute as proposed by the commissioners is as follows:

Section 2-503. Holographic Will. A will which does not comply with Section 2-502 is valid as a holographic will, whether or not witnessed, if the signature and the material provisions are in the handwriting of the testator.

The comment by the commissioners on the holographic will statute is as follows:

> This section enables a testator to write his own will in his handwriting. There need be no witnesses. The only requirement is that the signature and the material provisions of the will be in the testator's handwriting. By requiring only the *material provisions* to be in the testator's handwriting (rather than requiring, as some existing statutes do, that the will be *entirely* in the testator's handwriting) a holograph may be valid even though immaterial parts such as date or introductory wording be printed or stamped. A valid holograph might even be executed on some printed will forms if the printed portion could be eliminated and the handwriting portion could evidence the testator's will. For persons unable to obtain legal assistance, the holographic will may be adequate.

The statutes (numbers next to state names indicate the section of that state's statutes) of each of the 23 states where holographic wills are valid are summarized, paraphrased, or quoted to give you a good idea of the laws of each state.

- Holographic wills are valid where the signature and the material provisions of the will are made in the handwriting of the testator in the following states:

Alaska	13.11.160
Arizona	14-2503
Colorado	15-11-503
Idaho	15-2-503
Maine	18A-2-503
Michigan	27.5123
Montana	91A-2-503
Nebraska	30-2328
New Jersey	3B-3-3
North Dakota	30.1-08-03
Tennessee	32-105
Utah	75-2-503
Wyoming	2-6-113

- When the entire body of the will and the signature are in the handwriting of the testator, it can be established by the evidence of at least three distinterested witnesses to the handwriting and signature of the testator, without subscribing witnesses:

Arkansas	60-404

- A will written entirely in the testator's handwriting and signed and dated by him is valid in the following states:

  California............Probate Code 53
  Louisiana..................C.C. 1588
  Nevada......................133.090
  Oklahoma.....................84.54
  South Dakota..................29-2-8

- A holographic will is valid if it is wholly written and subscribed by the testator in the following states:

  Mississippi.....................91-5-1
  Virginia......................64.1-49
  West Virginia..................41-1-3

- A will wholly written by the testator is valid in:

  Texas...............Probate Code 60

For those who reside in these states the holographic will is entirely adequate, and they are easy to write.

Nuncupative Wills

A nuncupative will is one that is not in writing, and exists only when the testator declares his will orally before witnesses. At early common law, it was not essential to the validity of a nuncupative will that the testator be ill, and there were no restrictions on the time of making it. To guard against the frauds for which oral wills seemed to offer so many facilities, provision was made in the original statute of frauds in England that a nuncupative will to be valid must be *made in the time of the last sickness*. The privilege of leaving a nuncupative will, it was generally held at that time, was to be exercised as a matter of necessity, not of choice.

In American courts, the cases dealing with what constitute a *last sickness*, within the meaning of the requirement that a nuncupative will must be executed when the alleged testator is in that condition, fall roughly into two categories: those that follow the doctrine that, to be in his *last sickness* within the meaning of statutes relating to nuncupative wills, a putative testator must have been *in extremis*, and those which do not require an *in extremis* condition as a condition to showing the alleged testator was in his *last sickness*.

The rationale supporting the first category of cases is that a nuncupative will is not good unless it is made by a testator when he is *in extremis*, or overtaken by sudden and violent illness, and has not time or opportunity to make a written will. If nuncupative wills can be permitted at all in case of chronic disorders, according to the reasoning, it could be only in the very last stage and extremity of them. A full statement of the rule is that to be valid, a nuncupative will must have been made when the testator was *in extremis*, or overtaken by sudden and violent illness, when he had neither time nor opportunity to make a written will.

The second category of cases are based upon the conclusion that it is not necessary to label an alleged testator's condition as *in extremis* to find that he was in his *last sickness* when he attempted a nuncupation. Perhaps most of these rulings inferentially reflect what some of them expressly declare, namely, that the term last sickness simply means the sickness from which the deceased did not recover. Some courts have said that to require the testator to have been *in extremis* is adding words to the statute. It has also been reasoned that a too strict interpretation of the term *last sickness* might compel that stage of final illness so close to death that testamentary capacity would be lost.

These difficulties tend to support the suggestion made in the case that one should not seriously rely upon nuncupative wills. A *gift causa mortis*, where one, in contemplation of death, delivers a gift to another person, might be more effective in many circumstances than a nuncupative will.

Chapter 3

Who Can Make a Will?

Your right to designate who will receive your property is dependent upon your possession of testamentary power and testamentary capacity. It is important to know and understand the distinction between testamentary capacity and testamentary power. Testamentary power is the right, by will, to pass property to others of your choosing; that is, what property can be willed and to whom it can be given. This right is granted by the state statutes. Before you can transfer property by will, it is necessary that you possess both testamentary capacity and testamentary power. Testamentary capacity relates to the competency to make a will. For the most part, if you have testamentary power and capacity, you can dispose of your property by will to such persons and for such purposes as you choose, provided, of course, that such disposition is not contrary to the law or public policy.

Testamentary Capacity

Any person of sound mind and disposing memory and of proper age can make a will disposing of real and personal property. This is called testamentary capacity and is regulated by state statutes. Variations in these statutory provisions covering testamentary age range from 14 years to 21 years.

The capacity to make a will is determined as of the time of the execution of the will. If capacity exists at the time you write your will, it should be valid. It does not matter that you might not have had the competency, or capacity, to write a will some years ago or that you might become incapacitated, or incompetent, sometime in the future. The important thing is that you had the capacity when the will was written. The issue of capacity or competency is a question of fact that will be determined by a court should a contest develop.

It is this possibility, however, which makes it extremely important for you to carefully follow these guidelines for the execution of a will. It is better to spend an extra 10 minutes properly executing the will than to spend an extra 10 years litigating the issue as to whether it was properly signed. In most states, all adults are presumed to have testamentary capacity, and the burden of proving the contrary is on the person who contests the will.

What Law Governs Testamentary Capacity?

As to personal property, the laws of the state in which you reside govern. As to real property, the laws of the state in which the real estate is located govern. Generally, the disposition of property after death is controlled by the state laws and not the federal laws.

Prisoners

Ordinarily imprisonment does not destroy the right to make a will. In most of the states, it is provided by the constitution or by statute that conviction of a felony does not mean a forfeiture of an estate.

Illiterates

An illiterate person can execute a valid will if it is shown that he knows and understands the contents of his will, and if he meets the ordinary requirements of testamentary capacity.

Aged Persons

Advanced age does not, in itself, prove the incapacity to make a will. Also physical and mental weaknesses, because of old age, do not prove incompetency. Where a contest occurs, however, these conditions will be considered along with other evidence, facts, and circumstances that surround the execution of the will.

Blind Persons

The fact that a person is blind does not affect his testamentary capacity. Particular care must be exercised in the execution of the will of a blind person to make certain that it accurately expresses his testamentary intention and that no imposition or deceit is practiced upon him.

Diseased Persons

Physical illness or infirmity does not render a person incapable of making a will. An invalid or a person physically weak or extremely nervous can designate who is to receive the property provided his mental capacity is not seriously impaired. Most ailments of the body to some extent affect the mind; but there is a vast difference between the mind distressed by physical pain and a mind that is devoid of reason. The mere lowering of mental vitality by physical suffering does not disqualify one from disposing of property.

Drug Addicts

Persons addicted to the use of drugs can dispose of their property by will. It must be shown, however, that this person had sufficient mind and memory to understand the nature of the property and the nature of the act at the time the will was executed.

Habitual Drunkards

Habitual or extreme intoxication does not in and of itself result in a person's incapacity. To invalidate a will there must be additional proof that at the time the will was executed the natural intelligence, memory, and judgment of the person writing the will were paralyzed or perverted because of the intoxication. Proof that the person was a habitual drunkard does not prove that person intoxicated at the time the will was written. It has been held that a person can be intoxicated and still possess sufficient capacity to execute a will; that is, if he is able to, and does comprehend the nature and effect of his act and recall the persons who are to receive the property.

Moral Depravity

Testamentary capacity is not dependent upon moral conduct. The fact that a person does not measure up to accepted moral standards does not invalidate a will so long as that person is sane and the will expresses a free intent and purpose.

Mental Capacity

Absolute soundness of mind is not essential for the valid execution of a will. Although it is not necessary that a person have an intellect measuring up to the ordinary standard of mankind, he must possess a certain amount of intelligence. The universal rule for the measurement of testamentary capacity is that the person must understand the nature of the instrument written, must be able to recollect who was designated to receive the property, must know the nature and extent of this property, and must be able to dispose of it according to a plan formed in his mind.

Insanity

Proof of insanity at the time a will is written nullifies the will. The degree of proof necessary to invalidate the will is difficult to determine in many cases. It is not medical soundness of mind that governs testamentary capacity but soundness of mind as defined by law. A court of law can declare a person insane and appoint a guardian for him. This alone is not conclusive proof of the incapacity to make a will. Neither is a person assumed to have testamentary capacity merely because the court decides that he or she no longer needs a guardian. A will, made by a person committed to an insane asylum, can be held valid if it can be shown that the will was written during an intelligible or lucid period.

Belief in spiritualism, mumbling incoherently, eccentricities and oddities are not automatic reasons for mental incapacity. The neglect of personal hygiene and clothing, or offensive and disgusting habits are not necessarily considered evidence of insanity. A person who is vacillating, stubborn, stingy, easily angered, and indifferent to relatives does not necessarily demonstrate mental incapacity.

Unreasonable or unnatural provisions, unequal distribution among next of kin, and gifts to persons other than the natural recipients of a person's property do not constitute mental weakness unless they are so gross or ridiculous that they show obvious insanity. A person of sound mind can execute a will from any sort of motive that suits him or her, whether it be love, affection, gratitude, partiality, prejudice, hate, or capriciousness. Mental capacity is a question of fact to be decided by the court based upon all the evidence related to the issue. Many court battles have resulted from this issue.

Insane Delusions

An insane delusion, or false mental belief or conception that usually ignores reason, might or might not be of sufficient intensity to constitute mental incapacity. It must be established that the delusion directly affected the person's writing and that the belief expressed by that person was in fact false. An insane belief or a mere figment of the imagination (a belief in the existence of something that does not exist and that no rational person, in the absence of evidence, would believe to exist) are examples of delusions that can render wills invalid. To invalidate a will, the delusion must be a belief that is the spontaneous product of a diseased mind, that comes into existence without reason or evidence to support it, and that is adhered to against reason and against evidence.

A violent and unjust prejudice will not invalidate a will unless it is founded on an insane delusion. In one court case, a woman mistakenly believed that her relatives were unfriendly to her. The judge said that if all mistaken beliefs were to be cataloged as delusions, few indeed would escape the stigma of insanity. In another case, the judge said that if such belief is manifestly erroneous and entered into the will to the unjust detriment of the natural objects of the decedent's bounty, such belief amounts to a delusion such as renders the decedent incapable of making a valid will. Mental incompetency is not shown by the bequest of a person's estate to charity simply because that person believed he could not otherwise reach heaven. No creed or religious belief, in so far as it pertains to life after death, can be regarded as a delusion. This is because there is no test by which this belief can be tried or its truth or falsity demonstrated. Neither can a person's erroneous views of the law be considered delusions that can render a will void. If a belief is rational, though mistaken, it is not an insane delusion.

Impaired Memory

A perfect memory is not a requisite to competency. A disposing memory has been defined as one in which a person can recall the general nature, condition, and extent of his property and his relations to those to whom he gives and to those from whom he withholds that property. Mere forgetfulness, failure to recognize acquaintances, or failure to recollect the names of friends has been held insufficient to establish mental incapacity. Failure of memory, unless complete or nearly complete, does not invalidate a will.

Statutory Requirements

Generally, under modern statutes, a person of sound mind and otherwise competent can dispose of his property according to his pleasure, unless in contravention of some statute or common law rule. The general power of testamentary disposition is founded on the assumption that a rational will is a better disposition than any that can be made by the law itself. Testamentary power involves a privilege under the law to make a will while testamentary capacity concerns the ability of the testator to make a will. By way of example, at common law, convicts and married women had the capacity to make a will, but were denied the power to make a will by the old common law rules. Furthermore, statutes still require certain age requirements before granting the power or right to make a will. Each state has a statutory requirement as to the age at which one is competent to make a will. The statutes vary from age 14 to 21. There is no rational explanation as to why a 14-year-old person in Georgia can legally make a will disposing of real estate while across the border in Alabama, one must be 18. It is, of course, obvious that many people under 21 years of age do not feel a strong need for a will; however, it is equally obvious that many people under the age of 21 might have an overriding need for executing a valid will. In all events, it is necessary to look to the specific statutes in each state to determine the legal age for making a will.

For 45 of the 50 states, the requirement is 18 years of age or older. Georgia is the only state that allows a person 14 years of age or older to legally execute a will. Alaska requires the age of 19 years or older. Three states define the age requirement with a term rather than a stated number of years: New Mexico (Majority), Vermont (Full Age) and Wyoming (Legal Age).

Chapter 4

Who Can Receive Property Under a Will?

The right to designate who receives property is a privilege granted to individuals by the various states. The states and the federal government have the power to tax the transfer of property. Taxes are levied on the transfer of assets and on those who receive the assets. Because a will is effective only upon death, the capacity of a legatee cannot be determined until that time. The capacity of a person receiving property at the time of death is ordinarily not destroyed by prior or subsequent incapacity. The law of the state in which real property is located governs the disposition of that real property by will. The law of the state in which the person who has been designated to receive that real property lives, governs the right to receive that property.

Husband and Wife

Most states have statutes that provide for dower, curtesy, or statutory share (that portion of a person's property allowed to the spouse by statute). The rights of dower, curtesy, or statutory share cannot be defeated by a will. A few states have recently abolished dower and curtesy but give a statutory share to the surviving spouse, which is the same result. Most states also provide for a widow's allowance, homestead, and other rights that cannot be defeated by a will. Subject to these statutory requirements, you can dispose of your property as you wish. If you become separated or divorced or your family situation changes in any way, it is very important that you review your will and change it accordingly. Most statutes provide that a divorce or marriage will change the effect of an existing will.

Adopted Children

If you have adopted someone, the adopted person can receive property through the will, and it makes no difference whether formal adoption has ever been completed. It is only necessary that you clearly state your intention to devise or bequeath property to the adopted person. If the child or adopted person is specifically named to receive property, or when it appears by necessary implication that this person was meant to receive property, the instrument will be upheld. The recent trend in the laws is to treat the rights of adopted children the same as natural children.

Illegitimate Children

An illegitimate child can be given property by means of a will. If the child is not specifically named in the will, however, it must be clear that it is your intention to have the child included.

Murderer of the Testator

The right of a murderer to receive property by will from his victim has been denied by both civil law and common law. But few state courts in this country have made definite decisions on this issue, and the few decisions that have been made are unclear. To some extent, cases in this category are decided primarily on the specific facts and circumstances in each case. The statutory trend in most states is that a person who feloniously and intentionally kills another person cannot inherit from that person. This is recommended by the Uniform Probate Code.

Attesting Witness or Spouse of Witness

Ordinarily, a person who witnesses and signs a will cannot be a beneficiary of that will. This rule had its origin in the old common law of England and has been adopted in many of the states. Under the old English "Statute of Frauds," a person who witnessed a will was found to be incompetent, and the will was declared void because of incompetence. The injustice of this rule to the other beneficiaries of the will as well as to the person writing it soon became apparent, and the statutes were enacted restoring the competency of the witness but rendering this witness incapable of receiving property under the will. This removed the possibility of biased testimony as a witness could receive no financial gain. This rule is the reason for the suggested practice of not having any beneficiaries act as witnesses to your will.

In some states it has been held that only subscribing witnesses (those who sign as witnesses to the will) are barred from benefiting under the will, and not those who merely testify at probate as to the execution of the will or the capacity of the person who wrote it. Many statutes provide that if a will can be proved valid without the testimony of the witness who is to receive property, that witness can receive the property even though he testified at probate. In some states the right of a beneficiary, who is an essential witness to the will, is not destroyed but this beneficiary, or witness, can receive only that share of the estate he would be entitled to receive if there were no will. The amount, however, is not to exceed the amount to be given under the will.

By statutory provision in some states, property given to the wife or husband of a subscribing witness is void. The trend of the law is to permit the intent of the person writing the will whenever possible. In conclusion, it is best to choose as subscribing witnesses persons who are known to be trustworthy, but who have no financial stake in your will, either for themselves or their family.

Creditor of the Testator

A creditor of the person writing a will is not prohibited from accepting property by will from his debtor. However, when a creditor is a beneficiary under a will of his debtor, the question naturally arises as to whether the legacy was intended by the person writing the will in satisfaction of the debt and whether the creditor's acceptance of the legacy should bar his right to present the debt as a claim against the estate. This is a serious and complicated problem, as evidenced by the fact that the courts are in disagreement as to a general rule. In effect, it is your situation as expressed by the terms of your will or the circumstances surrounding its execution that governs. In the absence of unusual circumstances, a creditor can receive property under a will and also enforce a claim against the estate. A properly drafted will can avoid any dispute in these situations.

Debtor of the Testator

If you leave property to a person who owes you money, a similar question arises as to whether the property so willed cancels the debt. In the absence of an intention to the contrary, the property willed to a debtor will not, as a general rule, cancel the indebtedness. The intent to use the willed property to cancel the indebtedness must be explicitly stated in the will, or it must be shown by competent evidence. In one case where it was obvious by the terms of the will the testator intended the debtor to be the primary receiver of the property, the debt was not canceled because no specific direction was given in the will.

The courts have held that the executor of a will can retain a sufficient amount of the estate property to satisfy any indebtedness of the estate. This rule is founded upon the principle that a debtor should not be allowed to receive his legacy while he retains possession of funds out of which his and other legacies are to be paid. A simple but specific direction in the will that a debt shall not be deducted from a legacy to the debtor is effective, and, conversely, a direction to deduct debts from the creditors' legacies is binding.

Corporations

A private corporation, being an artificial person, is generally qualified to receive property under a will. The right of a corporation to receive personal property by will is unquestioned, and a bequest to a corporation for the future is valid. In most states, a corporation is permitted to take and hold real estate for the purpose for which it was incorporated.

Municipal Corporations

As a general rule, a municipal corporation is capable of receiving a bequest either for its own use or in trust for a specific and proper purpose. A city, county, town, or school township have all been held proper beneficiaries under a will. Also, the United States is considered a corporation and can take property by will. Even a community in a foreign country can be a beneficiary under a will when permitted by the laws of that country to receive such property. The trend under most modern statutes is to permit almost any entity or person to receive property under a will.

Unincorporated Bodies

For the reason that property can be given only to persons capable in law of holding property, it is generally held that an unincorporated association may not take property by will; it is not a separate "entity" from its members. In some states an unincorporated association may be given either personal or real property. Sometimes a gift to an unincorporated body has been upheld as a gift to its incorporated parent body; this and other devices are used by the courts to comply with the intentions of the testator.

Disinheriting

Subject to your spouse's marital rights or to the terms of a valid contract you have with your spouse, you can, in most states, disinherit any or all of the persons who would have a claim to your estate in case there was no will. Although a parent ordinarily has the right to disinherit his children for any reason whatsoever, most of the states have provided by statute that the intention to disinherit a child must be clear.

By reason of the statutes, the omission of a child from a will is presumed to have been unintentional or because of a mistake or forgetfulness. In some states extrinsic evidence to prove the intention to disinherit a child is admissible, while in other states the intention must appear in the contents of the will. It is not essential that any specific provision be made in the will as long as the child is either named or it can reasonably be implied that he was not forgotten.

Attorney Who Drafts Will

Most courts hold that a gift of property to the attorney who drafts your will presumes an improper or undue influence. This presumption is based upon the fact that people usually have a great deal of confidence, trust, and faith in their attorneys. The drafting of the will presents an opportunity and a temptation for the attorney, and this alone justifies the presumption. The presumption is one of fact and might be contested by competent evidence. Other courts simply hold that it violates professional ethics or that it is otherwise wrong as against public policy.

Executor or Trustee

The executor of a will can receive property under the will; however, the bequest should be given to him clearly as an individual and not as executor, since it might otherwise be presumed that the gift is because of his capacity. Although it is generally stated that a bequest is given to a person as executor and not by name, or where the bequest is given on the condition that the person enters upon and fulfills the duties of executor, the courts will presume that the legacy was given in a representative capacity and not the individual, and therefore was intended to be in place of compensation. Bequests to a trustee of a living trust have been generally upheld as valid, and are authorized and are approved by most modern state statutes.

Chapter 5

What Happens if You Die without a Will?

It might not be accurate to say that everybody needs a will, but every adult who has any assets or property should have one. While one of the most important items in a will is to designate who shall receive your property, an equally important item is to designate who shall not receive your property. If you do not have a will that appoints an executor (personal representative) to administer the estate, the court will appoint one. This can result in unnecessary delays. An appointed administrator is usually required to post a bond, a process that is both expensive and time-consuming. In addition to the expenditure of unnecessary bond premiums, the estate is charged with legal fees for the attorney who handles the procedural activities. Moreover, your family might not like the administrator appointed by some judge. A properly prepared will that appoints an executor and waives bonds would eliminate these delays and expenses, and avoid the potential for a strange judge appointing a stranger to administer your estate.

If the appointed administrator is required to sell the assets or property that belong to the estate because no will or legal provisions for the disposition of that property have been made, court authorization is first needed. Then, the administrator is probably required to obtain an appraisal of the property value. These proceedings are also time-consuming and expensive, and quickly add to the attorney fees and court costs. A properly prepared will can avoid these expenses, delays, and inconveniences.

If minors are involved, the court might need to appoint a legal guardian to protect the children's interest. In many cases, a court has appointed a *guardian ad litem* to represent the interests of a minor child to engage in litigation or disputes with the child's own mother. You might not be able to avoid all conflicts by appointing your own guardian, but your judgment about your own family is likely to be superior to that of some unknown judge. Further delays, expenses, and attorney fees result from these proceedings and could be avoided with a properly prepared will.

In addition to unnecessary expenses, delays, and inconveniences, there is a more important reason why a will is needed. If you die without a will, your property and assets will be distributed to those persons designated in the statutes of your state regardless of your wishes or desires and wholly aside from the needs of your family members. The following examples indicate the kind of difficulties intestacy can generate:

Example 1: Suppose you are a man, age 35, married to a woman, age 34, whom you love. You have two children, 8 and 5. Your mother and father are living. You have four brothers and two sisters all of whom you love. Your mother-in-law, age 67, is a battle-ax and you dislike her. You have an estate in excess of $800,000, and you have given your wife jewelry, furs, and other gifts from time to time. You have no will. On a vacation trip you have an accident and you and your two children are instantly killed. Your wife dies two weeks later; she has no will. Your mother-in-law will get it all.

Example 2: You are a woman, age 34, married to a man, age 36. You have no will, and your husband has no will. You are separated from your husband and have no children. You dislike your husband and hate his mother. A divorce action is pending. Your mother, age 72, inherited $700,000 from your father who died one year ago. Your mother dies and leaves her entire estate to you. Five days later you die in an accident and two weeks later your husband dies in a bar room brawl. Because of the failure to have estate plans or wills, most of the estate will probably be used to pay estate taxes, probate costs, and attorney fees. Your mother-in-law will get the balance, if any!

Example 3: Your best friend, age 25, married young, and is now getting a divorce from a man she hates. She is temporarily living with a man whom she expects to marry after the divorce is final. Her new friend has given her a new car, a condo in the mountains, and many other gifts. Her mother and father were recently killed in a plane crash, leaving her with a large estate. Three days before the divorce is granted, she dies from injuries sustained when she fell from a riding horse. Her estate, estimated to be in excess of $1,000,000 will go to the husband she doesn't like.

Although these examples might seem remote to you, similar situations have happened. Why take the chance? The thought that your situation could never be that tragic does not exclude the possibility of it happening to you. If you want to hear about other real cases read any newspaper any day. Suppose none of it ever happens to you. You still need a will. The costs of probate is high, but the "shocking" cases are almost always caused by people who fail to properly plan their estates. A recent survey revealed that 87½% of the adults in America do not have a will. Do you?

One who dies without a will is referred to as *intestate*. The status or condition is called *intestacy*. When this occurs the property owned by the decedent (intestate) is passed to "heirs" pursuant to a statutory process referred to as *descent and distribution* or *intestate succession*. The state statutes govern the distribution to the persons designated in the statutes. The descent and distribution or intestate succession statutes are enacted by the state legislatures based upon the assumption that most people want their estate to go to certain persons, usually close relatives. These assumptions might or might not comply with your own personal desires or wishes. In general, most statutes give priority or preference to spouses and children, lineal descendants, parents, brothers and sisters and their lineal descendants, and other collateral kindred. If none, then the property escheats to the state.

It would be unduly burdensome, and inappropriate, to list all the state statutes on descent and distribution or intestate succession because they vary greatly from state to state, and are subject to change from time to time. It is helpful, however, to review the relevant provisions of the Uniform Probate Code. The Uniform Probate Code is not necessarily the statutes in any state, but it is a model code prepared by the National Conference of Commissioners on Uniform State Laws. This Commission is composed of lawyers, judges, law professors, business people, and others who seek to make state laws more uniform.

The Uniform Probate Code

The following provisions are taken from the Uniform Probate Code, PART II, titled intestate succession. This is not necessarily the law of any particular state, but is a model code suggested for uniformity in state laws.

Section 2-101. Intestate Estate

Any part of the estate of a decedent not effectively disposed of by his will passes to his heirs as prescribed in the following sections of this Code.

Section 2-102. Share of the Spouse

The intestate share of the surviving spouse is:

(1) if there is no surviving issue or parent of the decedent, the entire intestate estate;

(2) if there is no surviving issue but the decedent is survived by a parent or parents, the first [$50,000], plus one-half of the balance of the intestate estate;

(3) if there are surviving issue all of whom are issue of the surviving spouse also, the first [$50,000], plus one-half of the balance of the intestate estate;

(4) if there are surviving issue one or more of whom are not issue of the surviving spouse, one-half of the intestate estate.

Section 2-103. Share of Heirs Other Than Surviving Spouse

That part of the intestate estate not passing to the surviving spouse under Section 2-102, or the entire intestate estate if there is no surviving spouse, passes as follows:

(1) to the issue of the decedent, if they are all of the same degree of kinship to the decedent they take equally, but if of unequal degree, then those of more remote degree take by representation;

(2) if there is no surviving issue, to his parent or parents equally;

(3) if there is no surviving issue or parent, to the issue of the parents or either of them by representation;

(4) if there is no surviving issue, parent or issue of a parent, but the decedent is survived by one or more grandparents or issue of grandparents, half of the estate passes to the paternal grandparents if both survive, or to the surviving paternal grandparent, or to the issue of the paternal grandparents if both are deceased, the issue taking equally if they are all of the same degree of kinship to the decedent, but if of unequal degree those of more remote degree take by representation; and the other half passes to the maternal relatives in the same manner; but if there be no surviving grandparent or issue of grandparent on either paternal or the maternal side, the entire estate passes to the relatives on the other side in the same manner as the half.

Section 2-104. Requirement That
Heir Survive Decedent for 120 Hours

Any person who fails to survive the decedent by 120 hours is deemed to have predeceased the decedent for purposes of homestead allowance, exempt property and intestate succession, and the decedent's heirs are determined accordingly. If the time of death of the decedent or of the person who would otherwise be an heir, or the times of death of both, cannot be determined, and it cannot be established that the person who would otherwise be an heir has survived the decedent by 120 hours, it is deemed that the person failed to survive for the required period. This section is not to be applied where its application would result in a taking of intestate by the state under Section 2-105.

Section 2-105. No Taker

If there is no taker under the provisions of this Article, the intestate estate passes to the state.

Section 2-106. Representation

If representation is called for by this Code, the estate is divided into as many shares as there are surviving heirs in the nearest degree of kinship and deceased persons in the same degree who left issue who survive the decedent, each surviving heir in the nearest degree receiving one share and the share of each deceased person in the same degree being divided among his issue in the same manner.

Section 2-107. Kindred of Half Blood

Relatives of the half blood inherit the same share they would inherit if they were of the whole blood.

Section 2-108. Afterborn Heirs

Relatives of the decedent conceived before his death but born thereafter inherit as if they had been born in the lifetime of the decedent.

Elective Share of Surviving Spouse

Section 2-201. Right to Elective Share

(a) If a married person domiciled in this state dies, the surviving spouse has a right to take an elective share of one-third of the augmented estate under the limitations and conditions hereinafter stated.

(b) If a married person not domiciled in this state dies, the right, if any, of the surviving spouse to take an elective share in property in this state is governed by the law of the decedent's domicile at death.

Section 2-203. Right of Election Personal to Surviving Spouse

The right of election of the surviving spouse may be exercised only during his lifetime by him. In the case of a protected person, the right of election may be exercised only by order of the court in which protective proceedings as to his property are pending, after finding that exercise is necessary to provide adequate support for the protected person during his probable life expectancy.

Spouse and Children Unprovided for in Will

Section 2-301. Omitted Spouse

(a) If a testator fails to provide by will for his surviving spouse who married the testator after the execution of the will, the omitted spouse shall receive the same share of the estate he would have received if the decedent left no will unless it appears from the will that the omission was intentional or the testator provided for the spouse by tranfer outside the will and the intent that the transfer be in lieu of a testamentary provision is shown by statements of the testator or from the amount of the transfer or other evidence.

(b) In satisfying a share provided by this section, the devises made by the will abate as provided in Section 3-902.

Section 2-302. Pretermitted Children

(a) If a testator fails to provide in his will for any of his children born or adopted after the execution of his will, the omitted child receives a share in the estate equal in value to that which he would have received if the testator had died intestate unless:

(1) it appears from the will that the omission was intentional;

(2) when the will was executed the testator had one or more children and devised substantially all his estate to the other parent of the omitted child; or

(3) the testator provided for the child by transfer outside the will and the intent that the transfer be in lieu of a testamentary provision is shown by statements of the testator or from the amount of the transfer or other evidence.

Note: The Uniform Probate Code is not necessarily the law of any particular state, but is a model code prepared for uniformity in state laws.

If you determine that you need a will follow the guidelines in this book and properly prepare and execute one. Every year millions of dollars are diverted from estates to legal fees, court costs, appraisal fees, executors' fees, guardian ad litem fees, expert witness fees, brokers' fees, taxes, tax penalties, interest payments, and other unnecessary expenditures rather than going to the family members as the decedent had wanted. The absence of a will can cause delays, inconvenience, personal sadness, and it frequently results in a miscarriage of justice. Fights, disputes, and lawsuits about who should have the property of family members is one of the tragedies inherent in the nature of mankind that seem to bring out the worst in everyone. All the hidden and repressed bitterness and hostility of every family member seem to surface at these times. You should not allow this to happen to your family. A properly prepared will can prevent most of the sadness and unpleasantness indicated by these examples. The apparent difficulty in preparing a will is not a sufficient reason to delay. You should carefully study your needs and immediately take definitive action. Do it now, even if you decide to employ a lawyer who might be appropriate.

A will is only one of many estate planning tools you need. If you appreciate the importance of a will, the significance of avoiding probate, discussed in Part 2, will emerge with the ineluctability of a syllogism.

Chapter 6

Federal Estate and Gift Taxes

Before the enactment of the Economic Tax Recovery Act of 1981 many estate planning and will writing efforts were directed toward the avoidance of federal estate and gift taxes. The new Tax Code provided much more liberal exemptions. Under current laws each estate has a $600,000 exemption. Moreover, there is an unlimited marital deduction. Therefore, over 99% of the estates will be exempt from such taxes. In view of these significant changes in the tax laws many people can write their own wills without having to worry about these tax problems.

The federal estate tax is imposed on the transfer of an individual's property at his death and on certain other transfers deemed to be the equivalent of transfers at death. The tax is imposed on the *taxable estate*. This is the value of the total property transferred or considered transferred at death. It is the gross estate reduced by various deductions, such as expenses, debts, claims, taxes and losses, marital deductions, charitable deductions, etc.

The tax is computed under the unified rate schedule applicable to both gift and estate taxes. Under the unified rate structure, lifetime gifts and transfers at death are taxed on a cumulative basis. Under the new tax code, estate taxes generally do not become a factor until the taxable estate exceeds the new exemption amounts. Remember that an unlimited amount can be transferred to a spouse, before or after death, without estate or gift taxes. This means that very few estates will have any estate and gift tax problems.

There is now a $10,000 annual exclusion for gifts, which means that any taxpayer can make gifts to any number of donees per year up to $10,000 each with no gift or estate tax liability.

The main category of property included in a decedent's gross estate is that in which the decedent had full or partial ownership when he died. Certain transfers made during the donor's lifetime, without adequate and full compensation, are taxed as part of the donor's gross estate for tax purposes because they are considered to be testamentary in nature. Gifts made within three years of the donor's death, gifts not taking full effect before the donor's death, and gifts that the donor might modify can be drawn into the donor's estate except to the extent that such transfers were made for adequate and full compensation.

Chapter 7

Writing Your Own Will

To review, the essential elements of a will are: a written instrument, a competent testator, an intent to dispose of property after death, and a will that is executed in accordance with statutory requirements. Obviously, a will contains much more than these elements and is limited only by the specific needs and desires of the person who writes it.

Although it is not absolutely essential to make a current inventory of your assets before writing your will, it is advisable to do so. The usual inventory includes such items as real estate, cash, automobiles, tangible personal property, stocks, bonds, insurance, profit sharing and pension funds, mutual funds, loans owed to you, business interests, and miscellaneous items. An essential part of estate planning consists of knowing the nature and extent of your current assets. After preparing your inventory of assets, you will find it much easier to make a decision as to what dispositions you wish to make in your will.

Do You Need a Lawyer to Write Your Will?

You do not need a lawyer to write a will unless you have significant tax problems or other legal entanglements. However, if you have any feelings of trepidation or uncertainty about your being able to write your own will, it is recommended that you consult with your attorney. Even if you decide to retain a lawyer for writing your own will, you can save money by completing your own inventory of assets and drafting your own version of your will to be reviewed by your attorney.

When Should You Retain a Lawyer?

Any time you are unsure about your own ability to properly write your own will, or having any legal problems, you should consult with your lawyer. It is much better to go to the trouble and expense of consulting a lawyer before you have a legal emergency than after it is too late. There are instances where it is advisable to consult a competent attorney in a timely fashion, to save money, time, embarrassment, and frustration.

The Main Parts of a Will

The following discussion will provide a checklist of the specific subjects usually found in a will and cover each of these subjects to the extent necessary to prepare a will. It will also provide examples of specific language to accomplish your objectives. It will present examples of typical wills that should cover all your needs. In drafting a will, use straightforward, commonly understood words and phrases. Avoid any terms that are ambiguous or subject to misunderstandings. If a phrase, sentence, or paragraph is not clear in its meaning when it is written, it surely might be misinterpreted later. Write simply but precisely in stating your intentions. Describe the specific results you want to accomplish. The more you know about wills and how the courts interpret them, the better prepared you will be to draft one of your own. The typical will usually contains the following parts:

- Introductory or Publication Clause
- Special Instructions
- Appointment of Executor, Executrix, Trustee, or Guardian
- General Gifts
- Specific Gifts
- Residuary Clause
- Execution of Will (Testimonium Clause)
- Simultaneous Death Clause Uniform Simultaneous Death Act
- Attestation Clause
- Signatures and Addresses of Witnesses
- Self Proof of Will

It is not mandatory that the contents be in any particular order, except that your signature and the signatures of the witnesses should be located at the end of the instrument. It is more convenient to have appointment of the executor on the first page, especially if you have a long will. If your will is longer than one page, it is good practice to sign in the margin on each page as well as on the last page. The signature at the end of the will is the only one that must be witnessed. The pages should be fastened together securely. It is recommended that the material be spaced so that the closing parts of the will—the testimonium clause, signature, attestation clause, and the witnesses' signatures—appear on the same page. Careful study of this book will better enable you to select, from the forms, the language necessary for a draft of your own will.

These basic will forms are used by most of the people who write wills. In fact, unless your estate exceeds the exemption amounts or you have some special estate problem, one of these basic wills is preferred. With the use of these forms and the additional provisions contained in the appendix, you should have no difficulty in drafting your will. If you are one of the few who has estate tax implications or other special situations, it is appropriate and proper to obtain professional assistance. If you decide to consult a professional, the knowledge gained from reading this book will save you and your professional consultant a lot of time, a factor that should lower fees.

Introductory or Publication Clause

The introductory or publication clause is the part that identifies the testator. It states that this is your last will and testament and that you are of sound mind and memory. It can be used to revoke all prior wills, if any. Here are the usual phrases used:

Example 1: *I, John Doe, of the City of _____, State of _____, being of sound and disposing mind and memory, do make, publish and declare this to be my Last Will and Testament, and hereby revoke all former wills and codicils by me made.*

Example 2: *I, John Doe, being of sound and disposing mind and memory and hereby intending to dispose of all property belonging to me at my death, of whatever kind and wherever situated, do make, publish and declare this to be my Last Will and Testament. . .*

Example 3: *I, John Doe, of _____(Address)_____, City of _____, State of _____, make this my Last Will and revoke all prior wills and codicils.*

Special Instructions

The law imposes a legal obligation to pay debts, and although it is not necessary to include a statement on the debts, such a statement is usually found in most wills. When a surviving spouse is obligated to pay the burial expenses of a deceased spouse, it can make a difference in the administration of the estate. This is a question you should discuss fully with your family when preparing your will. It is unnecessary to give specific directions about burial instructions, but this is another question you might wish to discuss with your family. Actually this should be done by separate written instructions and not as a part of your will. Because of the high costs associated with a typical funeral, many people now give specific directions to avoid excessive expenses. Instructions for cremation and donation to research foundations seem to be the current trend among people in this country. The typical provisions are:

Example 1: *My executor, hereinafter named, shall give my body a burial suitable to the wishes of my relatives and friends, and pay all of my funeral expenses, together with all my just debts, out of the first moneys coming into my estate.*

Example 2: *I direct that I be interred in a plot owned by me in _____ cemetery in the City of _____, State of _____, more particularly known as, ____(legal description)____ and that a suitable headstone be erected and inscribed upon said lot. The total cost of my funeral including the headstone shall be upwards of _____ Dollars, and for the purpose of providing for the perpetual care of said plot in said cemetery I hereby give, devise and bequeath to said cemetery, its successors and assigns the sum of _____ Dollars.*

Example 3: *It is my wish and I direct that my body shall be cremated after my death.*

Appointment of Executor, Trustee, or Guardian

Who should you appoint as executor of your will? Who should be appointed guardian of minor children or trustee of any trust you might establish? These are important questions and should receive careful consideration. The answers to these questions will depend entirely upon your own particular situation. The following general rules and suggestions will be helpful.

If you have a relatively small estate, you might wish to designate your spouse, a close relative, or a good friend to be the executor, the guardian of your children, or the trustee of your trusts. If there are no extensive business activities involved, no complicated real estate transactions, and no other major complications, these appointments are generally satisfactory and usually result in no difficulties and might reduce the amounts incurred for administration expenses. If a relatively large estate consists primarily of liquid assets or assets that easily can be converted to liquid assets, such appointments are also satisfactory. Moreover, the more family members do in the probate of an estate, the more the savings of probate expenses and attorney's fees.

Where an estate has a substantial interest in an active business necessitating active participation, complex partnership interests, extensive real estate holdings, or other assets that require active management and participation, it is advisable to appoint someone with business experience.

If you have minor children, or close relatives who are minors or otherwise unable to handle their own business affairs, you can set up a trust and designate a trustee to administer the trust until the beneficiaries become adults. The same general principles apply to the appointment of a guardian with the exception that when possible and appropriate, it is usually preferable to have an adult relative appointed guardian of very young children. You cannot always assume that the guardian of your minor children will be your surviving spouse. Simultaneous deaths are not uncommon. These questions should be carefully considered, and you will want to discuss them with your family. Your personal choice usually will be better than an appointment made by some judge who might not know you or your relatives.

After making these appointments, select alternates as successors to these appointments. There is no assurance that the person you designate at first will be able to act, or that the designated person will survive you. You should also carefully consider whether to waive bonds. This is generally recommended to save costs and expenses assuming, of course, that you have confidence in your appointees. Some suggested forms follow.

Example 1: *I hereby appoint Tom Doe of the City of _____, State of _____, and The First National Bank of __(city, state)__, executors of this my Last Will and Testament.*

Example 2: *I hereby appoint Tom Doe of the City of _____, State of _____, executor of this my Last Will and Testament, and direct that no bond or other undertaking be required of him for the faithful performance of the duties of his office.*

Example 3: *I appoint Tom Doe Executor hereunder and if he shall fail to qualify, or having qualified shall die, resign, or cease to act as Executor, then I appoint John Jones to act hereunder. No Executor named herein shall be required to give bond.*

Example 4: *(Guardian) If it shall be necessary to appoint a guardian for any minor child of mine, I appoint Tom Doe as such guardian. If he shall fail to qualify, or having qualified, shall die, resign, or cease to act as such guardian, then I appoint John Jones to serve as such guardian.*

General Gifts

General legacies are usually in money, but can be in other forms of personal property.

Example 1: *I give and bequeath to Mark Doe the sum of Fifty Thousand Dollars ($50,000.00).*

Example 2: I give and bequeath to Mark Doe fifty (50) shares of common stock of A.T. & T.

Specific Gifts

Specific gifts are particular personal property that is specifically designated; for example, items as jewelry, antiques, art objects, and other tangible objects.

Example 1: I give and bequeath my white pearl pin to my son, Tom Doe.

Example 2: I give and bequeath any automobile I might own at the time of my death to my son, Tom Doe.

Residuary Clauses

The residuary clause can be a very important part of a will—or it can be of no significance. That is, if there is nothing left in the estate it is of no significance. On the other hand, if a person has a large estate, the residuary clause would cover the disposition of all of the estate not specifically treated in the other provisions of the will. In the event a beneficiary of a general or specific bequest predeceases you that property would generally become a part of the residuary estate.

Example 1: All the rest, residue, and remainder of my property, real, personal, and mixed, at whatever time acquired by me and wherever situated, I give, devise, and bequeath to _____ *(name)* .

Example 2: I give the residue of my estate to my wife Jane.

Simultaneous Death Clause

What if you carefully prepare a will and you and all the beneficiaries in your will die simultaneously in a plane crash? What if you and your spouse own a house as joint tenants with right of survivorship (JTWROS) and both of you die simultaneously in a flood of machine gun bullets from a terrorist? Suppose none of these events occur, but you die a natural death and the next day the primary beneficiary in your will dies? Suppose you have a large estate, no will, and you and your closest relative, the person who would inherit your estate under the state statutes, dies simultaneously when a cruise ship on which you are taking a pleasure trip, sinks. What happens?

These hypothetical cases dramatize the importance of planning for such contingencies, but what happens if your primary beneficiary dies two weeks after you, or two months, or six? It is impossible to forsee all of the contingencies that could have a significant bearing on the results of your estate planning, but the death of your beneficiaries at or near your death is one that you should consider and address as best you can.

In the absence of a provision in your will covering simultaneous deaths, the laws of your state would apply. The Uniform Simultaneous Death Act, adopted in whole or in part in all but two states, is a model code recommended by the National Conference of Commissioners on Uniform State Laws. The model code provides as follows:

Uniform Simultaneous Death Act

An Act Providing for the Disposition of Property Where There Is No Sufficient Evidence that Persons Have Died Otherwise than Simultaneously, and to Make Uniform the Law with Reference Thereto.

Section 1. No Sufficient Evidence of Survivorship

Where the title to property or the devolution thereof depends upon priority of death and there is no sufficient evidence that the persons have died otherwise than simultaneously, the property of each person shall be disposed of as if he had survived, except as provided otherwise in this act.

Section 2. Survival of Beneficiaries

If property is so disposed of that the right of a beneficiary to succeed to any interest therein is conditional upon his surviving another person, and both persons die, and there is no sufficient evidence that the two have died otherwise than simultaneously, the beneficiary shall be deemed not to have survived. If there is no sufficient evidence that two or more beneficiaries have died otherwise than simultaneously and property has been disposed of in such a way that at the time of their death each of such beneficiaries would have been entitled to the property if he had survived the others, the property shall be divided into as many equal portions as there were such beneficiaries and these portions shall be distributed respectively to those who would have taken in the event that each of such beneficiaries had survived.

Section 3. Joint Tenants or Tenants by the Entirety

Where there is no sufficient evidence that two joint tenants or tenants by the entirety have died otherwise than simultaneously the property so held shall be distributed one-half as if one had survived and one-half as if the other had survived. If there are more than two joint tenants and all of them have died the property thus distributed shall be in the proportion that one bears to the whole number of joint tenants.

The term *joint tenants* includes owners of property held under circumstances that entitled one or more to the whole of the property on the death of the other or others.

Section 4. Community Property

Where a husband and wife have died, leaving community property, and there is no sufficient evidence that they have died otherwise than simultaneously, one-half of all the community property shall pass as if the husband had survived [and as if said one-half were his separate property], and the other one-half thereof shall pass as if the wife survived [and as if said other one-half were her separate property].

Section 5. Insurance Policies

Where the insured and the beneficiary in a policy of life or accident insurance has died and there is no sufficient evidence that they have died otherwise than simultaneously the proceeds of the policy shall be distributed as if the insured had survived the beneficiary [except if the policy is community property of the insured and his spouse, and there is no alternative beneficiary except the estate or personal representatives of the insured, the proceeds shall be distributed as community property under Section 4].

Section 6. Act Does Not Apply if Decedent Provides Otherwise

This act shall not apply in the case of wills, living trusts, deeds, or contracts of insurance, or any other situation where provision is made for distribution of property different from the provisions of this act, or where provision is made for a presumption as to survivorship which results in a distribution of property different from that here provided.

Note that this is not necessarily the law of any state; it is a model code to promote uniformity among the state laws. You should review the specific state statutes of your own state or the states in which the will might be probated or affected.

The statute of your state is not enough! It relates only to simultaneous deaths, and expressly provides in section 6 that you can make your own decisions "in the case of wills, living trusts, deeds, or contracts of insurance . . ."

It is recommended that you include in your will a simultaneous death clause along with a conditional survivorship clause in which a beneficiary must survive by 30, 60, 90, or 180 days. It is unfortunate to have an estate churned through the "probate system" twice within a short period of time. Indeed, once is too much! See Part 2 on how to avoid probate with respect to some, or all, of your assets.

Example 1: *If any beneficiary and I should die in a common accident or disaster, or if any beneficiary dies within (30, 60, 90, 180) days of my death, then all the provisions of this will shall take effect as if such beneficiary had in fact predeceased me.*

Example 2: *In the event that any beneficiary under this my will and I shall die under such circumstances that there is no sufficient evidence that we died otherwise than simultaneously, such beneficiary shall be deemed to have predeceased me.*

Execution of Will

The courts do not have the power to add to, or subtract from, the statutory requirements that govern the signing of a will. As the testator, your intention in this regard is also of no importance. You must comply with the requirements of your state statute.

The written will must be signed in some way by you and, to be valid, must be witnessed by competent persons. The only allowable exceptions are the rather unusual procedures previously mentioned (holographic wills and nuncupative wills).

You can personally subscribe your name, make your mark, have another person write your name for you, or have another person guide your hand or affix your fingerprint. Practically any court will hold that the will is valid if you affix your mark instead of write your name. The signature by a third party is sufficient if made in your presence, at your direction, and you assent to and adopt such signature as your own. If you are physically unable to sign your name, you can seek assistance from another person to help you write your name. As long as you participate in the act of signing your name and adopt it as your signature, the will is valid.

Frequent reference has been made to the signing of a will in accordance with statutory requirements. It is essential that you strictly comply with the requirements of any statute that might govern the disposition of property. Take precautions when signing your will to avoid the mistakes that have generated will contests in the past.

Here is a recommended procedure to follow in the execution and attestation of a will.

Prepare the final draft of the will, preferably on a typewriter or other printing facility, with an original and one or more copies. Type the attestation clause in the proper place. Allow ample space for your signature and the signatures of the witnesses. Number the pages and bind them together firmly. Make certain that you thoroughly understand the meaning of every part of the will.

Bring the witnesses together. Three witnesses will satisfy the requirements in all states except Louisiana. The witnesses should not be beneficiaries under the will or spouses of a beneficiary.

Inform the witnesses that the document before them is your last will. It is not necessary or even desirable that they be allowed to read it. Then you should state that you are about to sign the will and request the witnesses to witness your signature.

Then, with all the witnesses observing your action, sign the will. Sign only the original; the carbon copies, as a matter of good practice, remain unsigned but conformed. After you sign the will say to the witnesses, "This is my signature and this is my will. Will you please sign as attesting witnesses?"

Next, have the witnesses read the attestation clause. Then, have each witness sign immediately below the attestation clause and write his address.

Neither you nor any of the witnesses should leave the room until all have signed the document. Each signature must be observed by you and all the other witnesses.

Now the document is a will. Place the signed original in a safe place where it is available to you and to the executor. Do not place it in a safety deposit vault because a court order might be required to get it out. The unsigned copies should be conformed by typing or writing in the information from the original and placed in a different safe place.

Three witnesses are required by the statutes of Vermont. All other states except Louisiana require only two witnesses. The holographic will, legal in 23 states, needs no witnesses.

It is ordinarily required by most of the statutes that the witnesses be competent or credible. A competent witness has been defined as a person who could, at the time of attesting to the will, legally testify in court to the facts to which he attests by subscribing his name to the will. Credible is ordinarily used in the same sense as competent.

Attestation Clause

While most states require only two witnesses to a will, it is desirable to have at least three. Witnesses who are permanent residents of your city are preferable and their addresses should always appear on the will.

The attestation clause is not, by legal definition, a part of the will. It follows the will and is the written and signed statement of the witnesses. Its use is strongly recommended because it is evidence that the will has been properly prepared. It serves as an authoritative memorandum to refresh the memories of the witnesses. It is a good practice to include a statement that all the statutory requirements have been complied with. It is also recommended practice to state the number of pages in the will. If there have been any erasures or corrections in the will (and there should not be), they should be referred to in the attestation clause making it clear that the erasures or corrections were made by you before you signed the will. Typical attestation clauses follow.

Example 1: The foregoing instrument, consisting of three (3) typewritten pages, including this page, was signed, sealed, published, and declared by the said John Doe as his Last Will and Testament, in the presence of each of us, who at his request and in his presence and in the presence of one another, subscribe our names hereto as witnesses on the day of the date hereof; and we declare that at the time of the execution of this instrument the said John Doe, according to our best knowledge and belief, was of sound and disposing mind and memory and under no constraint.

Example 2: Signed, sealed, published, and declared by John Doe, the above named testator, who appears to us to be of sound and disposing mind and mem-

ory, as and for his Last Will and Testament in our presence, and we, at his request, in his presence and in the presence of each other, have hereunto subscribed our names as witnesses this _____ day of _____, 19 _____.

Self Proof of Will

A procedural device for the easy proof of wills has been adopted in most states. This procedure is recommended by the Uniform Probate Code and will probably be adopted by all states in the future. It is a further modernization and simplification of the probate procedures. It can be used as proof of a will without having to call in witnesses to do so after death, except in cases of contested wills. The self proof of a will can be made when the will is being written or subsequent to that time. As the testator, your acknowledgment of the will and the affidavits of the witnesses are made before an officer who is authorized to administer oaths. That person's authority is evidenced by the certificate attached to or following the will. This procedure is not required or necessary, but it is recommended that you use it if a notary public or other authorized official is available at the execution of the will. It might save a great deal of time, expenses, and effort, and it adds to the formality of the will.

A suggested form of the Self Proof of Will acknowledgment is as follows:

Self Proof of Will

STATE OF _____
COUNTY OF _____ ss
We, , , , and , the testator and the witnesses respectively, whose names are signed to the attached or foregoing instrument, were sworn and declared to the undersigned officer that the testator signed the instrument as his last will, that he signed, and that each of the witnesses, in the presence of the testator and in the presence of each other, signed the will as a witness.

_____   _____
Testator   *Witness*

                                                        _____
                                                        Witness

                                                        _____
                                                        Witness

Subscribed and sworn to before me by _____, the testator, and by _____, _____, and _____, the witnesses on the _____ day of_____, 19_____.

My Commission Expires:

_____   _____
                                                        Notary Public

An *acknowledgment* is a public declaration or formal statement of the person executing an instrument made to the official authorized to make the acknowledgment, that the execution of the instrument was his free act and deed. It is written evidence of an acknowledgment that generally states and declares that the person named in the document was known to the official and appeared before him and acknowledged the instrument to be his act and deed. An *affidavit* is a written statement made voluntarily and sworn to or affirmed before a person legally authorized to administer an oath or affirmation. As a general rule, any person who has knowledge of the facts sworn to in the writing can make an affidavit.

As a general rule, officers authorized to take acknowledgments include judges, clerks of court, notaries public, commissioners, and justices of the peace. Each state has a statute that makes these designations. In foreign countries the authorized officials usually include judges of a court of record, diplomatic counselors or commercial agents of the United States, and notaries public. Certain designated military personnel have authority to administer oaths for purpose of military administration, including military justice, and to act as notary and United States Consul in the performance of all notarial acts to be executed by members of the armed forces.

Miscellaneous Clauses

There are a number of other items that might be appropriate for certain wills. Each is examined in detail in the following sections.

Forgiveness of Debts

If you wish to forgive a specific debt owed to you by a person whom you designate as a beneficiary under your will, make a specific statement in the will of this intention. If you intend for the debt to be deducted from the legacy, state such an intent in the will.

Example: I give and bequeath to Mark Manning the sum of Five Thousand ($5,000.00) Dollars. I release and discharge said Mark Manning of any and all outstanding debts and interest thereon due me from him at the time of my death, and direct that the said Five Thousand ($5,000.00) Dollars be paid to the said Mark Manning in full, without any deduction on account of such indebtedness.

Common Disaster Clause

It is depressing enough to contemplate your own death, but the remote possibility of common disasters should be considered in the preparation of your will. Common disasters or simultaneous deaths are unfortunate, but it is equally unfortunate to see an estate shrink in size by being probated two or three times within a few years. It is one of the primary objectives of a good will to avoid unnecessary taxes and administration expenses. A common disaster clause or simultaneous death clause, as in the following examples, can help achieve this objective.

Example 1: *If any beneficiary and I shall die in a common accident or disaster, or if any beneficiary dies within 30 (60, 90) days of my death, then all the provisions of this will shall take effect as if such beneficiary had in fact predeceased me.*

Example 2: *In the event that any beneficiary under this my will and I shall die under such circumstances that there is no sufficient evidence that we died otherwise than simultaneously, such beneficiary shall be deemed to have predeceased me.*

Codicils

A codicil is an instrument that either adds to, or changes, an existing will. A codicil, to be valid, must meet all the statutory requirements of a will. In most instances, a codicil is merely a temporary change of a will until the testator has time to rewrite the entire will. Significant or extensive changes usually should not be made by codicil. It is recommended that you prepare a new will instead of relying upon codicils unless there is some compelling reason not to rewrite the will. For example, if a person is nearing senility or incapacity it is not recommended to write a new will, but to make a codicil for any changes. In most other instances, it will be as easy to write a new will as to write a codicil.

Revocation of Wills

To revoke a will means to annual it in whole or in part. A revocation can be expressed by virtue of a revocation clause contained in a later will or implied by reason of an inconsistent disposition of property in a later will. Under some statutes, a change in the circumstances of the testator subsequent to the execution of the will might constitute a revocation by operation of law. This emphasizes the importance of reviewing your will periodically, or after any significant change in your circumstances, to assure yourself that your will meets with your desires and intention. Upon being revoked, a testamentary provision ceases to exist, and is inoperative as if it had never been written.

A will can be revoked by tearing it up, cutting, burning, cancellation, erasure, obliteration, and any other physical act that essentially destroys the will so long as the acts are intended by you, the testator, as a revocation. A will can be revoked by operation of law, or as it is sometimes called *revocation implied by law*. Such a revocation can result from certain circumstances not specifically mentioned in the statutes that prescribe the proper methods of revocation. The doctrine is that the revocation of a will can be implied by certain changes in your family, domestic relations, your property, or one of the beneficiaries of your will. By these actions the law infers or presumes that you intended to make the change. The intended change can be either total or partial. The rule is based on the theory that by reason of such changes subsequent to the date of the will, you have acquired new moral duties and obligations. Subsequent marriage or divorce can have a significant change in the will. The death of the sole beneficiary in effect abrogates the will. Changes in the character of the estate will change the effect of a will. The birth of additional children could have an effect on an existing will.

Although most people rarely revoke a will without immediately preparing another, it is important for you to be familiar with the changes imposed by law so you will be in a position to prepare your own will and change it from time to time to meet your special needs.

Checklist

The final step in being able to draft a will is to assemble all of the facts and information about your estate, family, and personal situation. This is very important because it clearly defines your personal situation and enables you to answer questions. The checklist at the end of the chapter is designed to assist you in collecting facts you need. As you compile the information and identify each item that should be covered in the will, you can turn to the forms and draft an appropriate provision to resolve the question.

Name of Testator (your name)
- Are you known by any other name?
- Have you used other names in the past?
- If a name change has occurred, are the legal papers in order?

Domicile
- Do you own or maintain a residence outside the state in which the will is to be executed?
- Should a definitive statement be made in the will as to your intent regarding domicile or residence?

Age
- Do the dates on birth certificates and insurance policies coincide?
- Is evidence of your birthdate sufficient for social security purposes?

Family
- Are you married, single, a widow, widower, or adopted?
- Any previous marriages?
- What are the names, addresses, age, and marital status of your children?
- Are there any adopted children?
- Are there any deceased children?
- Do you intend to disinherit any of your children?

- Are any provisions to be made for children born after your death?
- Are any provisions to be made for individuals who claim to be your children?
- Have advancements been made to any of the children?
- If so, are they to be deducted from the gifts to the children?
- Are your parents living?
- Do you want to provide for them?
- Do you want to provide for any grandchildren?
- Do you want to provide for any other relatives?

Guardian

- Do you want a guardian to be appointed for your minor children?
- If so, who shall be appointed?
- Is the guardian to be required to give bond?
- What provision should be made for the support of your children?

Funeral Instructions

- Do you have a preference as to how your body should be disposed of?
- Are any provisions regarding cemetery lot, tombstone, and upkeep of the cemetery lot to be provided for in the will?

Prior Wills and Codicils

- Do you have copies of prior wills and codicils?
- Are all prior wills and codicils to be revoked?
- Have you made provisions to destroy any prior wills?

Debts

- Do you have any existing debts?
- Do you have any liability, such as surety on a bond, pledge to any charity or the like, etc.?
- Are debts to be paid from any specific property?
- What property is mortgaged or has other liens?
- Is mortgage or lien to be paid by the person or persons who receive your property, from the general estate, or from a particular fund?
- What property is to be sold first to pay any debts of the estate?
- If a gift is made to a creditor, is it to be in payment of your indebtedness or an addition thereto?

Debts Owed to You

- Are any debts to be canceled?
- Are special provisions to be made for their payment?
- If a legacy is given to one who is indebted to you, is the debt to be deducted from that legacy?

Husband and Wife

- Was an antenuptial agreement made?
- Are gifts to be in lieu of dower or curtesy?
- Are gifts to stop if the surviving spouse remarries?
- Are family living expenses to be provided during the period of time when the estate is being settled?

Property Owned by You

- Is there any property in your name that belongs to someone else?
- What is to be done with your property that is held as an agent or trustee for another?
- What property is to be specifically bequeathed or devised and to whom?
- What is to be done with your business, if any?
- What property is held jointly?
- Have you created any living trust?
- Have you any future or contingent interest? If so, how is it to be disposed of?
- Real Property:
  - ☐ What real property do you own?
  - ☐ Is the property owned in fee simple?
  - ☐ Has any real property been bought or sold on contract for deed?
  - ☐ Is any of this property mortgaged?
  - ☐ If mortgaged, is the devise to be subject to the mortgage?
  - ☐ Is there any real property located outside the state where you live?
  - ☐ What real property is to be specifically devised and to whom?
  - ☐ In whose name is the title to your family home?

- Personal Property
  - ☐ What specific items are to be bequeathed and to whom?
  - ☐ What money legacies, if any, are to be made and to whom?
  - ☐ How are personal effects to be disposed of?
  - ☐ Are any particular stocks, bonds, or mortgages to be specifically bequeathed? To whom?

- Partnership Property
  - ☐ Are you a member of any partnership?
  - ☐ Are there articles of partnership?
  - ☐ What provision is to be made as to the disposition of the interest in the partner and partnership?

Residuary Clause

- What shall be done with the balance of estate after all bequests have been paid or devised or real estate made or trusts set up and all debts paid?

Trusts

- Is any of your property to be left in trust?
- Who is to be the appointed trustee?
- What is to be done if the trustee dies, resigns, or is unable to act?
- To whom is the income to be paid and how is the principal to be distributed?

Conditional Gifts

- Are any gifts to be conditional?
- Are any provisions to be made for disinheriting persons who might contest the will?

Charities

- What gifts, if any, are to be given to charities?
- What gifts, if any, are to be given to servants, employees, or other persons?

Executor

- Who is to be the executor?
- Are provisions made if the executor dies or refuses to act as such?
- Will the executor be required to give bond?

Limitations on Wills

Each state has various statutory limitations on the making of wills. For example, as previously discussed, one must be of sound mind, be an adult, usually 18, and a beneficiary who murders a testator cannot receive property under the will. As discussed later, all property of a testator who uses the various methods for avoiding probate passes outside the will. There are a number of other statutory and constitutional provisions that vary from state to state that affects the transfer of property under a will. While these items vary from state to state, there are certain general items usually covered by most states, and some of these are listed below.

Joint Ownership

Where title to property is held in joint names with right of survivorship, the property passes outside the will automatically as a matter of law. In other words, the legal effect of such ownership is that automatically upon the death of one of the joint owners, the property—as a matter of law—passes to the survivor or survivors. Thus, this is sometimes referred to as a *substitute will* in the sense that there is no probate of such property. More specifically, these methods and techniques are more popularly referred to as *avoiding probate*, discussed later. Typically, these include titles taken in joint names with right of survorship. In some states this is called *community property* when taken in the names of husbands and wives. In other states it is called *estates by the entirety* when taken in the names of spouses.

State Statutory and Constitutional Rights

In many states, the statutes and constitutions also provide that surviving spouses, as a matter of law, have certain rights that cannot be defeated by a will. This is typically one-half, one-third, or some other percentage of the estate of a decedent. These rights typically have been called dower or curtesy, statutory rights, homestead rights, or simply elective rights. Moreover, some states statutes provide for a family allowance in the probate of estates that might be in conflict with, or overrides the provisions of a will. These rights are sometimes an option or *elective* right in the sense that, under some statutes, it is necessary to make a formal claim to obtain those rights. These rights, of course, can be waived. In other situations, for example, constitutional provisions for homestead rights, might be self-executing. In the case of elective rights the statutes give a spouse an elective right to *take against the will*, which means that the surviving spouse can elect to take the statutory share no matter what the will provides. This might be of considerable importance to those who do not recognize the legal difference between a separation and a divorce. For example, in a situation where a married couple separate but do not obtain a divorce, each spouse should be aware that the statutory rights obtain until termination of marriage by a divorce.

Divorce and Marriage

In most states, either a marriage or divorce automatically modifies the legal effect of a will. For example, upon a marriage each spouse automatically has the statutory elective rights. Upon divorce, the right is lost as a matter of law. For those community property states see the discussion in Part 2.

Witnesses and Spouses of Witnesses

Under some statutes neither witnesses nor spouses of witnesses are allowed to benefit from a will. Thus, it is important for you to avoid using a witness who is a beneficiary in your will, or a spouse of a beneficiary.

Birth of a Child after Execution of Will

If a person has a child born after the execution of a will, most statutes provide that the new child shall have a statutory share of the estate. This is another item that can alter or modify the legal effect of a will. The legislature in many states passed this statute on the assumption that most people would have included a child born after making a will if it had been called to their attention. This points out the importance of your reviewing your estate plans frequently to take care of changing circumstances in your family and estate.

As a general rule, one can disinherit almost anyone other than those items mentioned in the respective state laws, for example, the elective rights of surviving spouses. Therefore, you should take into consideration any statutory or constitutional limitations in the preparation and execution of your will.

One of the objectives of this book is to make the preparation of a will so simple that one can change it each time family changes occur, rather than trying to anticipate all kinds of changes that can occur in our lives. Review your estate planning frequently to make sure you have a will based upon your current situation.

Federal and State Estate and Gift Taxes

If you are not already disenchanted with all the so-called limitations on the making of a will, there remains one other that we all should try to avoid in the planning of our estates: Uncle Sam's big pocket and your state *inheritance or estate taxes.* While treatment of these topics is beyond the scope of this book, you should be aware of the problems presented even though the tax laws seems to change every time Congress or the state legislature meets.

Under current federal tax laws, each estate has a $600,000 federal tax exemption, and there is an unlimited marital deduction. This means that the first $600,000 of each estate is exempt from federal estate and gift taxes and there is no tax on property left to a spouse. Thus, over 99% of the estates will be exempt from such taxes.

The federal estate tax is imposed on the transfer of an individual's property at his death and on certain other transfers deemed to be the equivalent of transfers at death. The tax is imposed on the taxable estate. This is the value of the total property transferred or considered transferred at death. It is the gross estate reduced by various deductions, such as expenses, debts, claims, taxes and losses, marital deductions, charitable deductions, etc.

The tax is computed under the unified rate schedule applicable to both gift and estate taxes. Under the unified rate structure, lifetime gifts and transfers at death are taxed on a cumulative basis. Under the tax code, estate taxes generally do not become a factor until the taxable estate exceeds the exemption amounts. Remember that an unlimited amount can be transferred to a spouse, before or after death, without estate or gift taxes. This means that very few estates will have any estate and gift tax problems.

There is a $10,000 annual exclusion for gifts that means that any taxpayer can make gifts to any number of donees per year up to $10,000 each with no gift or estate tax liability.

The main category of property included in a decedent's gross estate is that in which the decedent had full or partial ownership when he died. Certain transfers made during the donor's lifetime, without adequate and full compensation, are taxed as a part of the donor's gross estate for tax purposes because they are considered to be testamentary in nature. Gifts made within three years of the donor's death, gifts not taking full effect before the donor's death, and gifts that the donor might modify can be drawn into the donor's estate except to the extent that such transfers were made for adequate and full compensation.

Some states do not have estate taxes, some do, and others have *inheritance* taxes that are imposed upon the persons who receive property from an estate. Review each state statute carefully to make sure you understand the laws of the states that might govern the administration of your estate. Discuss with professional estate planners estate planning to avoid these taxes.

Reasons for Having a Will

1. To give your property to those you choose—not as directed by a state statute without regard to your wishes or the needs of your family.
2. To direct who shall not inherit your property.
3. To protect your family and those you love.
4. To appoint the person you want to administer your estate.
5. To appoint a guardian for minor children, if needed, rather than leaving it to some probate judge you don't know.
6. To avoid litigation and disputes about your estate.
7. To save time and money in the administration of your estate.
8. To avoid delays in the administration of your estate.
9. To avoid unnecessary bond premiums and legal fees by waiving statutory requirements for bonds.
10. To avoid the excessive and unnecessary costs, delays, expenses, and aggravation of intestacy.
11. To avoid estate taxes by good estate planning.
12. To ensure peace of mind in knowing that your family is protected.

Questions and Answers
About Writing Your Own Will

1. What happens if I die without a will? Your assets will be distributed in accordance with the state statutes of descent and distribution—probably not as you would have chosen. The probate court probably will appoint a personal representative, guardian of minor children, if needed, and bonds will probably be required as provided in the state statutes. These proceedings usually generate additional attorney fees and other probate expenses. In addition to higher legal fees and probate costs, it will probably take longer to probate the estate than if you had prepared a will.

2. What is a will? An instrument executed by a competent person in the manner prescribed by statute, whereby he makes disposition of his property to take effect on and after death.

3. Where should I keep my will after it is completed? The signed original should be placed in a safe place where it is available to you and your personal representative. Do not place your will in a bank safety deposit vault because a court order might be required to get it out after your death. The unsigned copies should be placed in a different safe place for information purposes.

4. Who should act as witnesses to my will? Any adult who is competent. A competent witness has been defined as a person who could, at the time of attesting to the will, legally testify in court to the facts to which he attests by subscribing his name to the will. Do not have a minor, or a beneficiary, or spouse of any beneficiary of the will act as witnesses.

5. Does my will have to be notarized? No. You have the option to have it notarized if you have a notary public available at the time of execution. This could save time and expenses in the probate process, and it is sometimes called Self Proof of Will.

6. What is Self Proof of Wills? It is an affidavit that easily provides proof of the will. The person making the will and all witnesses acknowledge the signing of the will. The affidavit is taken before an officer who is authorized to administer oaths—usually a notary public. The person's authority is evidenced by the certificate attached to or following the will. This procedure is not required or necessary, but it is recommended that you use it if a notary public or other authorized official is available at the execution of the will.

7. How can I change or cancel my will? By writing a new will and expressly revoking the old one; by tearing it up, cutting, burning, cancellation, erasure, obliteration, and any other physical act that essentially destroys the will so long as the act is intended by the testator as a revocation. Also by codicil.

8. How do lawyers charge fees for writing wills? Usually on an hourly basis, anywhere from $100 to $300 per hour.

9. How much of an estate is exempt from federal estate and gift taxes? $600,000 each. There is an unlimited marital exemption that means that one can leave any amount to a spouse without any federal estate or gift taxes.

10. Who should I appoint as Personal Representative? Generally a spouse, relative, or close friend. Some states require the representative to be a resident of the state. Some people prefer to appoint a bank or trust company or a lawyer; however, this is quite expensive.

11. Who can I cut out of my will? In general you can disinherit anyone including children, but the intention to disinherit a child must be clear, and marital rights of a spouse might not be defeated by will.

12. What is a holographic will? A will written, dated, and signed in the handwriting of the testator (the person making the will). It needs no witnesses. This form of will is valid in the states listed in Part 1.

13. Do witnesses have to read the will? No. And they don't need to know what is in it. They should read and understand the attestation clause before signing as a witness.

14. Do I need a lawyer to prepare my will? No, not unless you have significant estate and gift tax problems or other legal entanglements.

Memo to My Personal Representative

The Personal History and Family Assets should contain most of the information needed in the administration of the estate, and burial directions. This memo is to assist in the probate proceedings, if any, of the estate. The following is a checklist of duties for the typical estate.

1. Give notice of death to all interested parties.
2. Check insurance coverage on all the decedent's estate.
3. Notify post office of any change of address.
4. Make copies of death certificate to be used in the probate of the estate.
5. Make copies of Last Will and Testament for beneficiaries, tax authorities, and others who might need one.
6. Call a family conference at which all interested parties can be advised of the fact available.
7. List contents of any safe deposit box.
8. Make a preliminary estimate of decedent's estate to determine what form of probate, if any, will be required.
9. Make an inventory of personal property and arrange for storage or distribution.
10. Obtain all checkbooks and bank records for financial information about the estate.
11. Account for all cash so it can be put to work, used for estate obligations, or distributed to the persons who are to receive it.
12. Assemble data on all property, if any, owned by estate that will not be a part of the probate process.
13. Notify utilities, charge accounts, credit cards, and other business accounts.
14. Assemble all personal records and tax records.
15. File tax returns for the estate, if needed.
16. Review any litigation, claims, or other controversies relating to decedent's property or property interests.
17. Collect all debts owed to the estate.
18. Pay all claims and expenses of the estate including probate costs and attorney fees, and make distribution to those entitled to the remaining assets. If informal probate of the estate is appropriate, consider doing it yourself without an attorney. Otherwise, if appropriate, employ an attorney to assist in the probate proceedings. Your understanding the *probate process* and knowing what to do can substantially reduce probate costs.

PERSONAL HISTORY AND FAMILY ASSETS FOR:

Your Name: _____

Address: _____

City: _____ State: _____ Zip: _____

Phone Number: _____

Date of Birth: _____

Place of Birth: _____

Nicknames: _____

Social Security Number: _____

Location of Birth Certificate, Marriage Certificate, Insurance Documents, Will

and other Papers: _____

_____

_____

_____

Information About Spouse

Name: _____

Address: _____

City: _____ State: _____ Zip: _____

Date of Birth: _____

Place of Birth: _____

Social Security Number: _____

Miscellaneous Information: _____

_____

_____

Information About Children

_____

_____

_____

_____

_____

_____

_____

_____

_____

_____

_____

_____

_____

Name and Addresses of Personal Representative and the Successors: ___

_____

Doctors, Lawyers, Accountants, Ministers, etc.: _____

_____

_____

_____

Assets: _____

_____

_____

Burial Instructions and Preplanned Arrangements: _____

_____

_____

Other Information: _____

_____

_____

_____

Chapter 8

Will Forms
and Alternative
Will Provisions

You can write your own will in the privacy of your own home without a lawyer and have the satisfaction of knowing your estate won't be distributed pursuant to a state statute, maybe even to strangers, but will go to those you designate. In this way, there will be no lawyers or others meddling in your private affairs. As previously mentioned, making your own will can also save money, time, frustration and a lot of the unnecessary aggravation of the probate system.

Before writing your will, read this entire book and then review the sections that pertain to your individual situation.

In preparing to write your own will make an inventory of your family assets, study the checklist, and discuss will writing with other members of your family. If the forms that follow do not contain exactly what you need, you should have no difficulty in selecting the form that most closely fits your situation and then take items from the other will forms, or from the list of alternative provisions, and be able to cover all your needs.

Two important considerations in writing your will are to spell everything out clearly, leaving nothing to chance, and periodically reviewing your will and other estate plans.

WILL FORM 1: Husband: Entire Estate to Wife If She Survives; Otherwise to Others

LAST WILL AND TESTAMENT
OF
_____
(name)

I _____*(name)*_____, a resident of _____*(city)*_____, _____*(state)*_____, hereby publish this my Last Will and Testament and revoke all prior wills and codicils.

1. *Special Instructions:* I direct that all my legal debts and funeral expenses be paid as soon as practicable after my death.

2. *Disposition:* I give my entire estate to my wife _____*(name)*_____ if she survives me. If she does not survive me, I give my entire estate (in equal shares) to the following beneficiary or beneficiaries who survive me: _____
_____.

3. *Trust for Minors, If Any:* The share of any beneficiary who shall be under the age of 18 (21, 25) years shall not be paid to such beneficiary but shall instead be held in trust to apply to his/her use all the income thereof, and also such amounts of the principal, even to the extent of all, as my Trustee deems necessary or suitable for the support, welfare, and education of such beneficiary; and, when he/she attains the age of 18 (21, 25) years, to pay him/her the remaining principal, if any. If any beneficiary for whom a share is held in trust should die before having received all the principal thereof, then upon his/her death the remaining principal shall be paid to his/her then living child or children, equally if more than one, and in default thereof, to my then living descendants, per stirpes.

4. *Executor:* I appoint my wife, _____*(name)*_____, Executrix hereunder and if she shall fail to qualify, or having qualified shall die, resign, or cease to act as Executrix, then I appoint _____*(name)*_____ to act hereunder. No Executrix or Executor named herein shall be required to give bond.

5. *Guardian:* If it shall be necessary to appoint a guardian for any minor child of mind, I appoint _____*(name)*_____ as such guardian. If he shall fail to qualify, or having qualified, shall die, resign, or cease to act as such guardian, then I appoint _____*(name)*_____ to serve as such guardian.

6. *Trustee:* In the event any trust shall come into existence under this will, I appoint _____*(name)*_____ as Trustee hereunder. If he shall fail to qualify, or having qualified, shall die, resign, or cease to act for any reason, I appoint _____*(name)*_____ to act as such Trustee. No Trustee named herein shall be required to give bond.

7. *Simultaneous Death Clause:* If any beneficiary and I should die in a common accident or disaster, or if any beneficiary dies within 30 (60, 90) days of my death, then all the provisions of this will shall take effect as if such beneficiary had in fact predeceased me.

IN WITNESS WHEREOF, I have hereunto set my hand this
_____ day of _____, 19_____.

(Signature)
_____

Testator name

Attestation and Witnesses

The foregoing instrument was signed, sealed, published, and declared by
the said ___*(name)*___ as his Last Will and Testament, in the presence of each
of us, who at his request and in his presence and in the presence of one another, subscribe our names hereto as witnesses on the day of the date hereof;
and we declare at the time of the execution of this instrument he, to our best
knowledge and belief, was of sound and disposing mind and memory and under
no constraint.

(Signature)
_____ residing at *(address)* _____
                            (city, state) _____

(Signature)
_____ residing at *(address)* _____
                            (city, state) _____

(Signature)
_____ residing at *(address)* _____
                            (city, state) _____

Self Proof of Will

I, ___*(name)*___, sign my name to this instrument this ___*(day)*___ day
of ___*(month)*___, 19_____, and being first duly sworn, to hereby declare to
the undersigned authority that I sign it willingly, that I execute it as my free
and voluntary act for the purpose therein expressed, and that I am 18 (14, 19,
21, 25) years of age or older, of sound mind, and under no constraint or undue
influence.

(Signature)
_____

Testator's name

We, ___*(name)*___, ___*(name)*___, and ___*(name)*___, the
witnesses, sign our names to this instrument, being first duly sworn, and do
hereby declare to the undersigned authority that the testator signs and executes
this instrument as his last will and that he signs it willingly, and that he executes
it as his free and voluntary act for the purposes therein expressed, and that
each of us, in the presence and hearing of the testator, hereby signs this will
as witness to the testator's signing, and that to the best of his knowledge the
testator is 18 (14, 19, 21, 25) years of age or older, of sound mind, and under
no constraint or undue influence.

(Signature)
_____

Witness (1)

(Signature)
_____

Witness (2)
(Signature)
_____

Witness (3)

STATE OF _____

COUNTY OF _____ ss

    Subscribed, sworn to and acknowledge before me by _____*(name)*_____, the testator, and subscribed and sworn to before me by _____*(name)*_____, _____*(name)*_____, and _____*(name)*_____, witnesses, this _____ day of _____, 19_____.

My Commission Expires:

(Signature)
_____

Notary Public
(address)

_____*(date)*_____

(city, state)

WILL FORM 2: Wife: Entire Estate to Husband
If He Survives; Otherwise to Others

LAST WILL AND TESTAMENT
OF
(name)

I _____*(name)*_____, a resident of _____*(city)*_____, _____*(state)*_____, hereby make
and publish this my Last Will and Testament and revoke all prior wills and codicils.

1. *Special Instructions:* I direct that all my legal debts and funeral expenses
be paid as soon as practicable after my death.

2. *Disposition:* I give my entire estate to my husband _____*(name)*_____ if he
survives me. If he does not survive me, I give my entire estate (in equal shares)
to the following beneficiary or beneficiaries who survive me: _____
_____.

3. *Trust for Minors, If Any:* The share of any beneficiary who shall be
under the age of 18 (21, 25) years shall not be paid to such beneficiary but shall
instead be held in trust to apply to his/her use all the income thereof, and also
such amounts of the principal, even to the extent of all, as my Trustee deems
necessary or suitable for the support, welfare, and education of such beneficiary; and, when he/she attains the age of 18 (21, 25) years, to pay him/her the
remaining principal, if any. If any beneficiary for whom a share is held in trust
should die before having received all the principal thereof, then upon his/her
death the remaining principal shall be paid to his/her then living child or children,
equally if more than one, and in default thereof, to my then living descendants,
per stirpes.

4. *Executor:* I appoint my husband, _____*(name)*_____, Executor hereunder and
if he shall fail to qualify, or having qualified shall die, resign, or cease to act
as Executor, then I appoint _____*(name)*_____ to act hereunder. No Executor named
herein shall be required to give bond.

5. *Guardian:* If it shall be necessary to appoint a guardian for any minor
child of mind, I appoint _____*(name)*_____ as such guardian. If he shall fail to qualify,
or having qualified, shall die, resign, or cease to act as such guardian, then I
appoint _____*(name)*_____ to serve as such guardian.

6. *Trustee:* In the event any trust shall come into existence under this will,
I appoint _____*(name)*_____ as Trustee hereunder. If he shall fail to qualify, or having
qualified, shall die, resign, or cease to act for any reason, I appoint _____*(name)*_____
to act as such Trustee. No Trustee named herein shall be required to give bond.

7. *Simultaneous Death Clause:* If any beneficiary and I should die in a
common accident or disaster, or if any beneficiary dies within 30 (60, 90) days
of my death, then all the provisions of this will shall take effect as if such beneficiary had in fact predeceased me.

IN WITNESS WHEREOF, I have hereunto set my hand this
_____ day of _____, 19_____.

(Signature)
_____
Testatrix name

Attestation and Witnesses

The foregoing instrument was signed, sealed, published, and declared by
the said _____*(name)*_____ as her Last Will and Testament, in the presence of each
of us, who at her request and in her presence and in the presence of one another, subscribe our names hereto as witnesses on the day of the date hereof;
and we declare at the time of the execution of this instrument she, to our best
knowledge and belief, was of sound and disposing mind and memory and under
no constraint.

(Signature)
_____ residing at *(address)*
_____
                              (city, state)
_____

(Signature)
_____ residing at *(address)*
_____
                              (city, state)
_____

(Signature)
_____ residing at *(address)*
_____
                              (city, state)
_____

Self Proof of Will

I, _____*(name)*_____, sign my name to this instrument this _____ day
of _____, 19_____, and being first duly sworn, do hereby declare to
the undersigned authority that I sign it willingly, that I execute it as my free
and voluntary act for the purposes therein expressed, and that I am 18 (14,
19, 21, 25) years of age or older, of sound mind, and under no constraint or
undue influence.

(Signature)
_____
Testatrix name

We, _____, _____ and
_____, the witnesses, sign our names to this
instrument, being first duly sworn, and do hereby declare to the undersigned
authority that the testator signs and executes this instrument as his last will
and that he signs it willingly, and that he executes it as his free and voluntary
act for the purposes therein expressed, and that each of us, in the presence
and hearing of the testator, hereby signs this will as witness to the testator's
signing, and that to the best of his knowledge the testator is 18 (14, 19, 21,
25) years of age or older, of sound mind, and under no constraint or undue
influence.

(Signature)
_____
Witness (1)

(Signature)
_____

Witness (2)
(Signature)
_____

Witness (3)

STATE OF _____

COUNTY OF _____ ss

Subscribed, sworn to and acknowledged before me by ____*(name)*____, the testatrix, and subscribed and sworn to before me by ____*(name)*____, ____*(name)*____, and ____*(name)*____, witnesses, this _____ day of _____, 19_____.

My Commission Expires:

(Signature)
_____

Notary Public
(address)

_____
(date)

(city, state)

WILL FORM 3: Married Person: Residue, After General Bequests, to Surviving Spouse; Otherwise to Issue with Provision for Minors

LAST WILL AND TESTAMENT
OF
_____
(name)

I ___*(name)*___, a resident of ___*(city)*___, ___*(state)*___, hereby do make and publish this will, hereby revoking all other wills by me heretofore made.

1. I direct that all my legal debts and funeral expenses be paid as soon after my death as might be practicable.

2. I give all my personal and household effects and automobiles that I own at the time of my death, including all insurance policies thereon, to my wife, ___*(name)*___, or, if she does not survive me, to such of my children as survive me, in equal shares, to be determined by my Executrix in her discretion. In case my wife shall predecease me, and any child of mine entitled to a share of the property disposed of by this paragraph shall be a minor at the time of my death, I authorize my Executrix, in her discretion, to retain such share for such minor during minority, or to deliver all or any part of such share in kind to such minor, or to the guardian of the property of such minor, or to the person with whom such minor might reside, or to sell all or any part thereof and to deliver the net proceeds of any such sale to such minor, guardian, or person with whom such minor might reside, in any case without requiring any bond, and to store any part retained and to pay all storage, insurance, and other carrying charges thereof out of any funds held for the benefit of such minor under this will.

3. I give to my ___*(relationship)*___, ___*(name)*___, if he/she survives me, the sum of $50,000.

4. I give to the ___*(organization)*___ for its general purposes, the sum of $50,000.

5. I give the residue of my estate to my wife, ___*(name)*___, or, if she does not survive me, to my children who survive me, in equal shares.

6. If any principal of my estate shall become distributable to a minor, my Executrix can in her absolute discretion pay over such principal at any time to the guardian of the property of such minor, or retain the same for such minor during minority. In case of such retention, my Executrix can apply such principal and the income therefrom to the support, maintenance, and education of such minor, either directly or by payments to the guardian of the property or person of such minor, or to the person with whom such minor might reside, in any case without requiring any bond; and the receipt of any such person shall be a complete discharge to my Executrix who shall not be bound to see to the application of any such payment. Any unapplied principal and income shall be

paid over to such legatee upon his/her attaining majority, or, if he/she shall die before attaining majority, to his/her estate.

7. I constitute and appoint ____*(name)*____, Executrix of this will, and direct that no bond shall be required of any Executrix or Executor.

IN WITNESS WHEREOF, I have signed this my Last Will and Testament this _____ day of _____, 19_____.

(Signature) _____

Testator's name

(This should be followed by the same attestation, witness, and Self Proof of Will as in Will Form 1.)

WILL FORM 4: Married Person;
Everything to Surviving Spouse
Conditioned on Time of Survivorship—
Otherwise in Separate Trusts for Children

LAST WILL AND TESTAMENT
OF
(name)
_____

I ____*(name)*____, a resident of ____*(city)*____, ____*(state)*____, hereby revoke my former wills and declare this to be my will.

1. I give, devise, and bequeath all of my estate, of whatever kind and description and wherever situation, to my wife, ____*(name)*____, providing she shall survive me by 30 (60, 90) days.

2. If my wife, ____*(name)*____, shall not survive me by 30 (60, 90) days, then I direct my Executor to divide my residuary estate into two equal parts, and to dispose of the same as follows:

A. *Trust for Daughter.* I give one of such equal parts to my Trustee, in trust, for the following uses and purposes: to take control and management thereof, and to invest and reinvest the principal and keep the same invested, and to receive the income therefrom, and, after paying the reasonable and proper expenses of the trust, to pay the income therefrom to my daughter, ____*(name)*____, during her life. Upon the death of my daughter, or, if she shall not survive me, then upon my death, my Trustee shall pay over the principal, as it shall then exist, to the issue of my daughter per stirpes; or, if no such issue shall then be living, then to those of my issue who shall then be living per stirpes.

B. *Trust for Son.* I give the other such equal parts to my Trustee, in trust, for the following uses and purposes: to take control and management thereof, and to invest and reinvest the principal and keep the same invested, and to receive the income therefrom, and, after paying the reasonable and proper expenses of the trust, to pay the income therefrom to my son, ____*(name)*____, until he shall attain the age of 30 (25, 18) years of age, and thereupon to pay over the principal to him as it shall then exist. In the event that my son dies before attaining the age of 30 (25, 18) years, or if he shall not survive me, then upon my death, my Trustee shall pay over the principal, as it shall then exist, to such persons and in such estates, interests, and proportions as my son shall, by his will admitted to probate, appoint; or, in default of such appointment, then to his estate.

3. I appoint my wife, ____*(name)*____, Executrix of this will. If my wife shall fail to qualify or cease to act, I appoint my brother, ____*(name)*____, Trustee of the trusts hereunder. If my brother shall fail to qualify or cease to act in any

of the foregoing capacities, I appoint my wife's sister, ____*(name)*____, in such capacity in the place and stead of my brother. I direct that none of these individuals shall be required to file a bond or other security in any jurisdiction for the faithful performance of his/her duties.

In Witness Whereof, I have hereunto set my hand and seal on the _____ day of _____, 19_____.

_____
(Signature)

Testator's name

(Attestation, Witnesses, Self-Proof of Will)

WILL FORM 5: Married Person—
One Half in Trust for Spouse;
Other Half in Trust for Parents

LAST WILL AND TESTAMENT
OF
_____
(name)

I _____*(name)*_____, a resident of _____*(city)*_____, _____*(state)*_____, hereby make, publish, and declare this to be my Last Will and Testament.

1. I hereby revoke all other wills by me at any time heretofore made.

2. I direct that my debts and my funeral expenses be paid as soon after my death as might be reasonably convenient, and I authorize and empower my Executors, in case any claim is made against my estate, to settle and discharge the same in their absolute discretion.

3. I give and bequeath all my household furnishings, furniture, jewelry, silverware, books, automobiles, wearing apparel, and all other personal effects which might be owned by me at the time of my death, together with all policies of insurance relating thereto, to my wife, _____*(name)*_____, if /she survives me.

4. A. I give, devise, and bequeath 50% of the residue of my estate to my Trustees, in trust, to collect and receive the income, and after deducting all expenses incident to the administration thereof, to pay the net income therefrom, in quarter annual installments, as nearly equal as possible, to my wife, _____*(name)*_____, during her lifetime. In addition, if in any calendar year, including the year in which my death occurs, the aggregate income of this trust shall be less than _____*(specific amount)*_____, there shall be paid to my wife out of the corpus of this trust, upon her request within the first three months of the succeeding calendar year, an amount of cash or property sufficient to make the total payments from this trust for such year, including income, equal in value to _____*(specific amount)*_____, but if such request is not make for any calendar year, no payments of corpus shall be made in any subsequent calendar year on account of the amount not so required.

B. I hereby grant to my wife, alone and in all events, the power to appoint by her will the entire remaining corpus of the trust, free of this trust, to her estate or in favor of any other person or persons.

C. If my wife predeceases me, or, if having survived me, she has not exercised by her will the power of appointment herein granted to her, I direct that 50% of the residue of my estate, or the remaining corpus of the trust for the benefit of my wife, as the case may be, shall be paid over absolutely to my issue, per stirpes, but, if there be none then living, to my parents, _____*(name)*_____ and _____*(name)*_____, equally, or entirely to the survivor of them, or if neither of them be then living, to the persons who would be entitled to inherit the same had I then died intestate owning such property.

5. A. I give, devise, and bequeath the remaining 50% of the residue of my estate to my Trustees, in trust, to collect and receive the income, and after deducting all expenses incident to the administration thereof, to pay the net income therefrom in quarter annual installments to my parents, in equal shares, for their lifetimes, and entirely to the survivor to them for the survivor's lifetime. In addition, if in any calendar year, including the year in which my death occurs, the aggregate income of this trust payable to each of my parents shall be less than _____*(specific amount)*____, there shall be paid to each of my parents, and to the survivor of them, out of the corpus of this trust, upon his or her request within the first three months of the succeeding calendar year, an amount of cash or property sufficient to make the total payments from the trust to each of them, and to the survivor of them, for such year, including income, equal in value to _____*(specific amount)*____, but if such request is not made for any calendar year, no payments of corpus shall be made in any subsequent calendar year on account of the amount not so requested.

B. Upon the death of the survivor of my parents, or at my death, whichever is later, I direct that the 50% of the residue of my estate, or the remaining corpus of the trust for the benefit of my parents, as the case might be, shall be paid over absolutely to my issue, per stirpes, but, if there be none then living, to my wife, _____*(name)*____, or, if she be not then living, to the persons who would be entitled to inherit the same had I then died intestate owning such property.

6. In the event of any emergency, my Trustees can, within their sole discretion, apply any portion of the corpus of any trust to the support and care of the beneficiary or beneficiaries then entitled to the income of such trust.

7. No person dealing with the Executors or Trustees shall be obligated to see to the application of any moneys, securities, or other property paid or delivered to them, or to inquire into the expediency or propriety of any transaction or their authority to enter into and consumate the same upon such terms as they might deem advisable.

8. I hereby appoint my friend, _____*(name)*____, Executor hereunder and if he shall fail to qualify, or having qualified shall die, resign, or cease to act as Executor, then I appoint _____*(name)*____ to act hereunder. No Executor or Executrix named herein shall be required to give bond.

9. I hereby appoint _____*(name)*____ as Trustee hereunder. If he shall fail to qualify, or having qualified, shall die, resign, or cease to act for any reason, I appoint _____*(name)*____ to act as such Trustee. No Trustee named herein shall be required to give bond.

IN WITNESS WHEREOF, I have hereunto set my hand and seal this day of _____, 19_____.

_____
(Signature)

Testator's name

(Attestation, Witnesses, and Self Proof of Will)

WILL FORM 6: Married Person:
Entire Estate to Spouse
or Child If Spouse Predeceases Testator

LAST WILL AND TESTAMENT
OF
(name)
_____

I ___*(name)*___, of ___*(city)*___, ___*(state)*___, make this my last will, and revoke all prior wills or codicils.

1. I direct that the expenses of my funeral be paid as soon after my death as might be practicable.

2. I give my entire estate to my wife, ___*(name)*___, if she survives me.

3. If my wife, ___*(name)*___, does not survive me, I give my estate, in equal shares to my ___*(number)*___ children, ___*(name)*___, ___*(name)*___, and ___*(name)*___. The share of any legatee who shall be under the age of 18 (21, 25) years, shall not be paid to such legatee but shall instead be held in trust to apply to his/her use all the income thereof, and also such amounts of the principal, even to the extent of all, as my Trustee deems necessary or suitable for the support, welfare, and education of such legatee; and when he/she attains the age of 18 (21, 25) years to pay him/her the remaining principal, if any. If any legatee for whom a share is held in trust should die before having received all the principal thereof, then upon his/her death the remaining principal shall be paid to his/her then living child or children, equally if more than one, and in default thereof, to my then living descendants, per stirpes.

4. In the event that my wife, ___*(name)*___, shall die with me in a common disaster or accident, or under such circumstances as might make it impossible or difficult to determine which of us died first (or within, 30, 60, 90 days after my death), I direct that my wife shall be conclusively deemed not to have survived me (or predeceased me).

5. I appoint my wife, ___*(name)*___, Executrix hereunder and if she shall fail to qualify, or having qualified shall die, resign, or cease to act as Executrix, then I appoint my brother, ___*(name)*___, and the ___*(Bank name)*___ of ___*(city)*___, ___*(state)*___, as Coexecutors hereunder. No Executrix/Executor named herein shall be required to give bond.

6. If it shall be necessary to appoint a guardian for any minor child of mine, I appoint my sister, ___*(name)*___, as such guardian. If my sister shall fail to qualify, or having qualified, shall die, resign, or cease to act as such guardian, then I appoint my ___*(relationship)*___, ___*(name)*___, in her place and stead.

7. In the event any trust shall come into existence under this will, I appoint my ___*(relationship)*___, ___*(name)*___, Trustee hereunder to serve without bond. If my ___*(relationship)*___, shall fail to qualify, or having qualified, shall die, resign,

or cease to act for any reason, I appoint such person as my _____*(relationship)*_____,
_____*(name)*_____, shall designate, by instrument in writing duly acknowledged,
as his substitute or successor. No Trustee named herein shall be required to
give bond.

(Signature)
_____

Testator's name

(Attestation, Witnesses, and Self-Proof of Will)

WILL FORM 7: Married Person:
Entire Estate to Spouse with Alternative Gifts
to Children If Spouse Predeceases Testator

LAST WILL AND TESTAMENT
OF
(name)

_____

I ____*(name)*____, a resident of _____*(city)*_____, County of ____*(county)*____, State of ____*(state)*____, being of full age and sound and disposing mind and memory, hereby make, publish, and declare this to be my Last Will and Testament, and I hereby revoke any and all wills by me at any time heretofore made.

FIRST: I direct that all my legal debts and funeral expenses be first paid out of my estate.

SECOND: After the payment of my legal debts and funeral expenses, I give, devise, and bequeath all of my estate, real, personal and mixed of every kind and nature whatsoever and wheresoever situated, to my beloved wife/husband, ____*(name)*____, absolutely and in fee simple, and in the event she/he predeceases me, I give, devise and bequeath all of my said estate to my children absolutely and in fee simple, in equal shares, and if any of my children not be living at the time of my death the share of any deceased child shall go to the issue per stirpes, of said deceased child, but if there be no such issue shall be paid to my issue, then living, per stirpes.

THIRD: I hereby nominate and appoint my beloved wife/husband ____*(name)*____, to be the Executrix/Executor of this my Last Will and Testament, and in the event of the death of the said ____*(name)*____, during my lifetime, or her/his incapacity or refusal to act, I nominate and appoint ____*(name)*____, of _____*(city)*_____, as Executrix/Executor. I hereby direct that neither ____*(name)*____ nor ____*(name)*____ shall be required to give any bond as such Executrix or Executor. (Appointment of Guardian and Trustee for minor children, if appropriate.)

IN WITNESS WHEREOF, I hereunto set my hand, and declare the foregoing instrument to be my Last Will and Testament.

Date this _____ day of _____ , 19_____.

(Signature) _____
Testator's name

(Attestation, Witnesses, and Self Proof of Will)

WILL FORM 8: Married Person:
Entire Estate to Spouse with Alternative Gifts in Trust
for Minor Children If Spouse Predeceases Testator

LAST WILL AND TESTAMENT
OF
(name)

I, _____*(name)*_____, residing at _____*(address)*_____, City of _____*(city)*_____, State of _____*(state)*_____, being of sound and disposing mind and memory, and considering the uncertainty of this life, do make, publish, and declare this to be my Last Will and Testament as follows, hereby revoking all other former wills by me at any time made.

FIRST: After my lawful debts are paid, I give, devise, and bequeath all my property, real, personal, and mixed, to my wife/husband outright, if she/he survives me.

SECOND, If my wife/husband, _____*(name)*_____, should predecease me, then I give, devise, and bequeath all my property, real, personal, and mixed, in equal shares, to my children, me surviving, subject, however, to the provisions of paragraph THIRD.

THIRD: If a child taking under the preceding clause is under the age 21 at the time of my death, then I give, devise, and bequeath the share of each such child to _____*(name)*_____, IN TRUST NEVERTHELESS, for the following purposes and under the following terms:

(1) to invest said share according to the law of the State of _____*(state)*_____;

(2) to pay the income and principal of said share to such child or for the benefit of such child, in the discretion of said Trustee;

(3) to accumulate the said income in his discretion and to pay the accumulated income to such child or for the benefit of such child, in whole or in part, as said Trustee sees fit;

(4) to pay accumulated income, if any, and the balance of the principal, if any, to such child when he or she reaches the age of 21. If such child dies before reaching the age of 21, then to pay said accumulated income, if any, and the balance of the principal, if any, to his/her estate.

FOURTH: In the event that my wife/husband, _____*(name)*_____, and I shall die under such circumstances that there is no sufficient evidence that we died otherwise than simultaneously, then my wife/husband, _____*(name)*_____, shall be deemed to have predeceased me.

FIFTH: I hereby appoint my wife/husband, _____*(name)*_____, to be Executrix/Executor of this my Last Will and Testament, to serve without bond. If she/he shall predecease me, I appoint _____*(name)*_____ to serve as Executrix/Executor without bond. I appoint ____*(name)*____ as trustee of any trusts created hereunder to serve without bond.

IN WITNESS WHEREOF, I have hereunto subscribed my name and affixed my seal this _____ day of _____, 19_____.

(Signature)

Testator's name

(Attestation, Witnesses, and Self Proof of Will)

WILL FORM 9: Married Person: No Children; Entire Estate to Spouse with Alternative Gifts to Brothers and Sisters

LAST WILL AND TESTAMENT
OF
(name)

I, _____*(name)*_____, of the city of _____*(city)*_____, County of _____*(county)*_____, State of _____*(state)*_____, being over the age of eighteen years, and of sound and disposing mind and memory, do hereby make, publish and declare this to be my Last Will and Testament, and hereby revoke all wills and codicils heretofore made by me at any time.

FIRST: I direct that all my just debts and funeral and testamental expenses be paid as soon after my decease as conveniently can be done.

SECOND: I give and bequeath to _____*(name)*_____ the sum of _____*(specific amount)*_____ Dollars ($_____).

THIRD: All the rest, residue, and remainder of my estate, real, personal, and mixed, of every kind and nature of whatsoever, and wheresoever located, I give and bequeath to my beloved wife/husband, _____*(name)*_____, absolutely and forever.

In the event, however, that my said wife/husband shall predecease me, or shall die simultaneously with me, or so nearly so that it cannot be determined which of us survived the other, then, in any of such events, all of the said residue to which she/he would have been entitled shall be divided into as many equal shares as there are brothers and sisters of mine living at my death and brothers and sisters of mine who have predeceased me leaving issue living at my death. One such share shall be paid over to each brother and sister of mine who is then living, and one such share shall be paid over to the issue, per stirpes, of each brother and sister of mine who has predeceased me leaving issue living at my death.

FOURTH: I hereby nominate, constitute and appoint my wife/husband, _____*(name)*_____, to be the Executrix/Executor of this my Last Will and Testament, and in the event of her/his death during my lifetime or her/his incapacity or refusal to act, I nominate, constitute, and appoint _____*(name)*_____ of _____*(city, state)*_____, as Executrix/Executor. I hereby direct that neither my said wife/husband, or the said _____*(name)*_____ shall be required to give any bond as such Executrix/Executor.

IN WITNESS WHEREOF, I have hereunto set my hand, and declare the foregoing instrument to be my LAST WILL AND TESTAMENT.

foregoing instrument to be my LAST WILL AND TESTAMENT.
Dated this _____ day of _____, 19_____.

(Signature)
_____
Testator's name

(Attestation, Witnesses, and Self Proof of Will)

WILL FORM 10: Widows and Widowers with Children: Entire Estate Outright to Children

LAST WILL AND TESTAMENT
OF
(name)
_____

I ___*(name)*___, declare this to be my will and revoke all former wills and codicils that I have made.

FIRST: All obligations of my estate shall be paid. These shall include all death taxes and deficiencies, interest and penalties thereon, assessed in any way by reason of my death, whether on property passing under my will or otherwise. As to death taxes assessed against my estate on property not passing under my will, I direct my Executor not to seek contribution from the recipient for his/her share of such taxes.

SECOND: I give all of my goods and chattels, including my household furniture and furnishings, automobiles, books, pictures, jewelry, watches, silverware, china, and wearing apparel in equal shares to my children who survive me.

THIRD: All the residue of my estate, real or personal, and wherever situated, including lapsed legacies and any property over which I might have a power of appointment, I give and devise per stirpes to my descendants who survive me.

FOURTH: I appoint ___*(name)*___ Executor/Executrix of this will, and I give him/her the following powers, authorities and discretions, to be exercised if he/she chooses, without order of court.

A. To sell at any time or times, at public or private sale, and to mortgage or lease, all or any part of the property, real or personal, of my estate, on such terms as he/she deems best;

B. To settle claims in favor of us against my estate as he/she deems best;

C. To distribute the residue of my estate passing under Paragraph THIRD to the distributees thereof either in cash or in kind, or partly in each, as he/she deems best;

D. To make, execute, and deliver any and all deeds, contracts, mortgages, bills of sale, or other instruments necessary or desirable in order to exercise the powers, authorities, and discretions granted in subparagraphs A through C.

If for any reason ___*(name)*___ does not act or continue to act as Executor/Executrix, then __*(name)*___ is appointed Successor Executor/Executrix with all of the powers, authorities, and discretions conferred on ___*(name)*___ as Executor/Executrix hereunder. Neither the Executor/Executrix nor the Successor Executor/Executrix shall be required to post bond for the faithful performance of his/her duties.

FIFTH: I appoint ____*(name)*____ guardian of the estate and of the person of any minor children of mine who survive me.

IN WITNESS WHEREOF, I have signed this will, consisting of ____*(name)*____ typewritten pages, the witnesses' certificate included, and on the margin of each page except this page I have signed my name for greater security, this _____ day of _____, 19____.

(Signature)
_____

Testator's name

(Attestation, witnesses, and Self Proof of Will)

WILL FORM 11: Unmarried Persons

LAST WILL AND TESTAMENT
OF
(name)

I, _____*(name)*_____, of the city of _____*(city)*_____, State of _____*(state)*_____, make this my last will, revoke all prior wills or codicils.

1. I direct that the expenses of my funeral be paid as soon after my death as might be practicable.

2. I give my entire estate to my mother, _____*(name)*_____, or, if she predeceases me, then to my father, _____*(name)*_____, or, if both predecease me, then to my _____*(relationship)*_____, _____*(name)*_____, and _____*(name)*_____, share and share alike.

3. I appoint my mother, _____*(name)*_____, Executrix hereunder, and if she shall fail to qualify, or having qualified, shall die, resign, or cease to act as Executrix, then I appoint my father, _____*(name)*_____, Executor hereunder. No Executrix/Executor shall be required to give bond.

4. If any beneficiary and I shall die in a common accident or disaster or under such circumstances that it is doubtful who died first, then all the provisions of this will shall take effect as if such beneficiary had in fact predeceased me.

IN WITNESS WHEREOF, I have hereunto set my hand this _____ day of _____, 19_____.

(Signature)
_____
Testator's name

(Attestation, Witnesses, and Self Proof of Will)

WILL FORM 12: Holographic Will (Handwritten)

LAST WILL OF _____ *(name)* _____

This is my will, and I revoke all prior wills. I give all my property to my wife/husband, _____*(name)*_____, if she/he survives me, and if she/he predeceases me, then I give my property to my children, share and share alike.

I appoint my wife/husband, _____*(name)*_____, Executrix/Executor of this will and waive all bonds. This will is written, dated, and signed by me in my own handwriting.

Date this _____ day of _____, 19____.

(Testator's Signature) _____

WILL FORM 13: Codicil

LAST WILL AND TESTAMENT
OF
_____
(name)

WHEREAS I, _____*(name)*_____, on _____*(date)*_____, 19_____, signed, sealed, declared, and published my Last Will and Testament in the presence of _____*name)*_____, _____*(name)*_____, and _____*(name)*_____, who signed the said will and testament as witnesses; and

WHEREAS, I am desirous of adding an additional bequest and devise in the said will, I, therefore, make and publish this codicil to said will not in conflict with this codicil.

1. I hereby give, bequeath, and devise to _____*(name)*_____, my daughter mentioned in my will, my solitaire diamond ring, and ten shares of stock in the _____*(company name)*_____, to be hers absolutely, without accountability in the distribution provided for in the residuary clause of my said will.

2. In the event _____*(name)*_____, my said wife/husband, after qualifying as Executrix/Executor marries or departs this life, then and in that event I appoint _____*(name)*_____, my son, sole executor of my will, in the place of his mother/father, conferring upon him generally the same powers in reference to my said estate as are conferred upon my wife/husband in my said will.

3. The special bequests and devises made to _____*(name)*_____, my wife/husband in the third paragraph of my original will, I intend and declare to be in lieu of dower/curtesy or statutory share in the event my wife/husband should elect to take under my said will.

IN WITNESS WHEREOF, I have signed and published this will on this _____ day of _____, 19_____.

_____
(Signature)
Testator's name

(Attestation, Witnesses, and Self Proof of Will)

WILL FORM 14: Revocation of Will

REVOCATION OF
LAST WILL AND TESTAMENT

WHEREAS, I, ___*(name)*___, on ___*(date)*___, 19____, signed, declared, and published my last will and testament in the presence of ___*(name)*___, ___*(name)*___, and ___*(name)*___, who signed the said will and testament as witnesses; and

WHEREAS, I am desirous or revoking said will and testament, I do, therefore, hereby revoke said will and testament (or any portion that the testator might desire to revoke) and I do hereby declare it to be null and void to the same extent as though I had never signed it.

IN WITNESS WHEREOF I have signed and published this Revocation of Will on this _____ day of _____, 19____.

(Signature) _____

Testator's name

(Attestation and Witnesses)

WILL FORM 15: Nuncupative Will
(Dictated to Notary in Louisiana)

LAST WILL AND TESTAMENT

Before me, _____*(name)*_____, clerk of the _____*(name)*_____ District Court in and for the Parish of _____*(parish name)*_____, duly commissioned and qualified as such, and ex officio notary public, in the presence of _____*(number)*_____ competent witnesses residing in the Parish of _____*(parish)*_____, State of Louisiana, _____*(testator name)*_____, a resident of _____*(city or parish)*_____, State of Louisiana, personally came and appeared and declared unto me, notary, in the presence of the undersigned witnesses, that he/she wished to make his/her last will and testament and that he/she wished me to receive his/her last will and testament; and he/she, the said testator/testatrix, dictated to me this his/her last will and testament in the presence of the witnesses; and I, notary, received it from his/her dictation and wrote down the same as it was dictated to me in the presence of the said testator/testatrix, and the witnesses, in the following words, to wit:

I, _____*(name)*_____, being of sound mind and knowing that life is precarious, wishing to make a proper disposition of my property in the case of my death, in the presence of the undersigned notary and witnesses do make and declare this my last will and testament, revoking all former wills and testaments whatsoever.

1. I desire that all my just debts be paid.

2. I give and bequeath unto my daughter, _____*(name)*_____, of _____*(city, state)*_____, the sum of _____*(specific amount)*_____ dollars.

3. I give and bequeath unto my son, _____*(name)*_____, of _____*(city, state)*_____, the sum of _____*(specific amount)*_____ dollars.

4. I give and bequeath unto _____*(name)*_____, of _____*(city, state)*_____, the sum of _____*(specific amount)*_____ dollars.

5. All the remainder of my property, whether real or personal, which I might leave at the date of my death, I give and bequeath unto my wife/husband, _____*(name)*_____, and make and appoint her/him the Executrix/Executor of this my last will and testament, and give her/him all rights to my estate from the moment of my death, and dispense with the necessity of any bonds.

This last will and testament of _____*(name)*_____, was dictated by her/him to me, notary, in the presence and hearing of the witnesses, and was reduced to writing by me, notary, as dictated.

I, notary, then read the above will to her/him in the presence of the witnesses, that she/he was entirely satisfied with the will, and she/he signed it in my presence and in the presence of the witnesses, and the whole was received, dictated, read, and signed at one time, without interruption and without turning aside to any other act.

This was done, read, and signed at the residence of the testator, in the Town and Parish of _____(parish)_____, State of Louisiana, on this the _____ day of _____, 19 ____.

(Signature) _____

Testator's name

(Signature) _____

Notary Public

(Attestation and Witnesses)

Optional Will Provisions

The following examples are representative of the most commonly used optional provisions appearing in wills. These provisions and adaptations of them, along with the variety of will forms preceeding this section, should cover about 99% of the specific situations one might encounter. If you are in that other 1%, you might wish to consult an attorney.

Executors to Hold Property for Minor Child

If any legatee under this will shall be a minor at the time of my death, I authorize my executors, in their sole and absolute discretion, as they might deem best, either to sell any of the property to which such minor might be entitled under this will, or to hold such property for him or her (without bond) until he or she reach the age of 18 (21, 25) years, or until such earlier time as my executors might deem proper to deliver such property to such minor or to such person (without bond) with whom such minor shall reside, for the benefit of such minor.

General Gifts

I give the sum of five thousand dollars ($5,000) to my friend, _____*(name)*_____, if he/she survives me.

Specific Gifts

I give to my son, _____*(name)*_____, and my daughter, _____*(name)*_____, share and share alike, per stirpes and not per capita, the real property owned by me at ___*(city, state)*___, which land is more particularly described as follows: *(address or information from deed)*.

Disinheritance of Heirs Not Named

I have intentionally omitted all my heirs who are not specifically mentioned herein, and I hereby generally and specifically disinherit each, any, and all persons whosoever claiming to be or who might be lawfully determined to be my heirs at law, except as otherwise mentioned in this will.

Omission of Any Person Except Spouse

I have intentionally omitted to mention, or to give anything to any person or persons other than my wife, _____*(name)*_____.

Bequest to Surviving Children

I give to my children who shall be living at the time of my death my entire estate, equally to be divided between them; and if any dispute should arise with respect to the division, I authorize my Executor to distribute the effects equally among my children.

Division Per Stirpes

I give ___(property description)___ to ___(name)___ and ___(name)___, their heirs, executors, administrators, and assigns, their descendants to take per stirpes and not per capita.

Division Per Capita

Should any legatee predecease me, leaving children surviving me, such children shall take per capita, share and share alike, and not per stirpes.

Gift of Automobiles and Furniture

I give to my wife, ___(name)___, all my automobiles and household furniture and effects together with any and all insurance policies thereon.

Gifts of Personal Effects and Household Goods

All my jewelry, clothing, personal effects, books, paintings, works of art, and all household goods and household furnishings of every description I give to ___(name)___.

Specific Devises

I give, devise, and bequeath to my wife, ___(name)___, if she survives me, in fee simple, the buildings and land located at ___(address)___, City of ___(city)___, State of ___(state)___. If my wife does not survive me, this gift shall lapse and the property described herein shall fall into and become part of my residuary estate.

I give and devise to my wife, ___(name)___, if she survives me, or if not, in equal shares to my children who survive me, their heirs and assigns forever, all real estate owned by me at the time of my death, including all buildings and improvements thereon, and all rights and other interests pertaining thereto.

I give and devise to my son, ___(name)___, and my daughter, ___(name)___, share and share alike, per stirpes and not per capita, the real property owned by me at ___(city)___, County of ___(county)___, State of ___(state)___, and further described as follows: ___(address or information from deed)___.

Specific Legacies

I give and bequeath to my wife, ___(name)___, if she survives me, all my furniture, furnishings, books, linens, silver, china, glassware, jewelry, wearing apparel, automobiles, and all other household and personal goods and effects.

To my daughter, ___(name)___, I give my diamond ring and my good watch. If my daughter does not survive me, this legacy shall lapse and become part of my residuary estate.

I give and bequeath of my law books, office equipment, and all property contained in my law office to my son, ___(name)___, if he shall survive me.

General Legacies

I give and bequeath the sum of $ _(specific amount)_ to ___(name)___ if he/she survives me, or if he/she does not, then per stirpes to those of his/her issue who survive him/her.

I give and bequeath the sum of $ ___(specific amount)___ to my friend, _____, if he/she survives me.

I give and bequeath $ ___(specific amount)___ to my sister, ___(name)___, of ___(city, state)___ payable from any funds I might have on deposit in any type of account in the _(bank or trust name)_____.

Testamentary Trust Clauses

All the rest of my estate, including property over which I have a power of appointment, I give, bequeath, devise, and appoint to my trustee in trust for the following purposes:

(1) My trustee shall hold, manage, invest, and reinvest the principal, shall collect the income therefrom and shall pay the net income therefrom to my wife during her life.

(2) My trustee shall pay to my wife from time to time such sums from principal as will in the discretion of my trustee permit her to maintain the standard of living to which she was accustomed during her lifetime. In making such invasions of principal my trustee shall not consider any other resources of my wife or any other sources of income.

(3) Upon the death of my wife or at my death if she should predecease me, my trustee shall pay or distribute the then principal of the trust to and among my issue who are then living in equal shares per stirpes, or if there are no such issue then living, my trustee shall pay or distribute the then principal of the trust to and among those of my nephews and nieces who are then living in equal shares per capita.

If my wife, ___(name)___, survives me, I give to my trustee the sum of $ ___(specific amount)___ in trust to pay the net income in semiannual installments to my wife for a period of ten (10) years following my death or until her remarriage or death before then. The trust shall terminate upon the happening of the first of these events to occur and the principal shall be paid over absolutely to my wife if she is then alive and unmarried or otherwise to my issue per stirpes.

I give ___(percent or all)___ of the residue of my estate to my trustees for the following purposes:

(1) The same shall be divided into two (2) equal shares, and one (1) share shall be held in trust for my son, ___(name)___, and the other for my daughter, ___(name)___.

(2) The income from each share shall be accumulated until the beneficiary thereof has attained the age of ___(number)___ ( ) years.

(3) The principal and accumulated income of each share shall be paid to the beneficiary thereof when he or she attains the age of ___(number)___ years.

Should either of my children predecease or die before reaching age
____*(number)*____, their share shall be added to the share of the survivor. Should
both my children predecease me or die before reaching age ____*(number)*____, then
one-half (½) shall be divided per capita amount those of my nephews and nieces
who are living at the death of the survivor of my (2) children, or at my death,
as the case might be.

Spendthrift Trust Clause

The income reserved to the respective beneficiaries of any trust created
by this will shall not be subject to anticipation, or to pledge, assignment, sale,
or transfers in any manner nor shall any beneficiary have power in any manner
to charge or encumber such interest, nor shall such interest be liable or subject
in any manner while in the possession of the trustee for the liabilities of any
beneficiary, whether such liabilities arise from his debts, contracts, torts, or
other engagements of any type.

No principal or income payable, or to become payable, in any trust created
by this will shall be subject to anticipation or assignment by any beneficiary
thereof, or to attachment by or to the interference or control of any creditor
of any such beneficiary, as to be taken or reached by any legal or equitable
process in satisfaction of any debt or liability of such beneficiary, prior to its
actual receipt by the beneficiary.

I direct that all legacies and devises and all shares and interests in my estate,
whether principal or income, while in the hands of my executor or trustees,
shall not be anticipated, alienated, or in any other manner assigned or transferred
by the legatee, devisees, or beneficiary, and such interest shall be for the sole
and separate use of the legatees, devisees, and beneficiaries, and shall be free
and exempt from anticipation, execution, assignment, pledge, attachment,
distress for rent, and other legal or equitable process that might be instituted
by, and on behalf of, any creditor or assignee of such legatee, devisee, or beneficiary, or his or her spouse.

Abatement and Preference Clauses

If my estate is insufficient to pay all bequests and devises, I direct that the
order of abatement shall be general legacies, specific legacies, and then specific
devises. All bequests and devises of the same class shall abate proportionately,
provided only that abatement of any legacy or devise to my wife shall not begin
until all other bequests and devises in the same class have been abated
completely.

If my estate is insufficient to pay all of the legacies in full, then I direct that
the legacies to my wife shall be first paid in full.

If my estate is insufficient to pay of the general legacies in full, I direct that
the general legacies be paid in the consecutive order in which they are set forth
in this will.

Business Interests

I direct my Executor/Executrix to discontinue and liquidate, as soon after my death as is practical, any business or business interests that I own at my death, upon such terms as in the discretion of my Executor/Executrix shall be in the best interests of my estate. In carrying out such liquidation, my Executor/Executrix can sell any such business or business interest as a unit or can sell the assets of any such business separately from time to time, and such sale or sales can be consummated at public sale or by way of negotiated sales, and in either case upon such terms of payment and credit as my Executor/Executrix shall determine.

I authorize my Executor/Executrix to continue any business that I own at my death for such period of time as in the discretion of my Executor/Executrix shall be in the best interests of my estate, without liability for any losses incurred in carrying on such business or for any depreciation in the value of any of the assets thereof. None of the general assets of my estate, however, shall be used or employed directly, or indirectly, in carrying on such business, nor shall these general assets become liable for any debts of such business. My Executor/Executrix can in his/her sole discretion, transfer all or part of the net assets of such business to a corporation organized by him/her in return for all or part of its capital stock, and in such event my Executor/Executrix can hold such corporate stock for such period of time as, in his/her discretion, shall be in the best interests of my estate, and shall have the power during such period to participate directly, or indirectly, in the management of this corporation.

Bequest of Business

I give and bequeath the goodwill and benefit of the business of _____*(company name)*_____, which I am now carrying on at _____*(city, state)*_____, and also all my capital and property that shall be employed therein at my decease and also the leasehold premises situated at _____*(address)*_____, wherein said business is now being carried on, for all my term and interest therein, unto my son, _____*(name)*_____, absolutely.

General Bequest of Items of Personal Property

I give and bequeath to _____*(name)*_____ all of my household furniture, rugs, paintings, works of art, ornaments, tapestry, silverware, plate, books, linen, china, glassware, and all other household goods and supplies that I own at the time of my death.

Bequest of Expenses for College Education

It is my will and desire that _____*(name)*_____ shall have the benefit of four (4) years of college education, and I direct that my trustee pay from my estate all expenses of attendance for four (4) years at a recognized college, said expenses not to exceed the sum of $ _____*(specific amount)*_____ dollars.

Bequest of Unpublished Manuscripts

To ____*(name)*____, all unpublished manuscripts, to be handled by her/him in accordance with instructions that I have given.

Bequest of Papers, Letters, and Documents

I give and bequeath to ____*(name)*____ all letters, papers, manuscripts, diaries, and other writings. This bequest, however, does not include legal documents, such as agreements, contracts, deeds, notes, or mortgages.

Devise of Family Home

If I own a house and plot of ground at the time of my death, which is being used by me and my wife as a family home, then I give, devise, and bequeath such house and plot of ground unto my said wife, subject, however, to any encumbrance or encumbrances thereon existing at the time of my death (or free and clear of any encumbrance thereon existing at the time of my death).

Part 2
Avoiding Probate

Chapter 9

Probate

Part 1 explained, with easy-to-follow instructions, how to write your own will, without a lawyer, and with full confidence in its legality. Part 2 explains what probate is, what is involved in probate proceedings, and how you can avoid it entirely by the use of the Revocable Living Trust and other probate avoidance methods and techniques. Estate planning is no longer a monopoly for lawyers. You can now do it yourself!

Probate is the legal process by which property and property rights are transferred from a decedent to others. From a time "from whence the memory of man runneth not to the contrary" the probate system has been dominated and controlled by lawyers and judges. The probate statutes, laws, and procedures have become fossilized, archaic, outdated, and out of step with the reality of our modern society.

Because of the antiquated laws, evolved by the judges and legislatures controlled by lawyers, and the resulting high costs of administration, extravagant legal fees, delays, court costs and other expenses, most citizens in this country have become disenchanted with the entire probate process and the mystique that enshrouds it. American citizens have been cast into a cloud of darkness as to how to intelligently plan an estate to avoid the abuses and scandals so frequently reported by the press.

A few years ago Americans became so disgusted with the probate scandals that something had to be done for their survival. Rather than having each generation being subjected to what the average citizen called the *probate rip-off*, where a large percentage of a family estate was taken away, the concept of avoiding probate by placing assets in trusts became an estate planning tool for those who resented the excessive charges, and the occasional embezzlement or outright theft by lawyers and judges. The cases from which these scandals arose were, for the most part, carefully orchestrated probate processes carried on routinely by the people who so completely controlled the probate system that it was very difficult to obtain any legal recourse. Moreover, an occasional impeachment of a probate judge or the disbarment of a crooked lawyer did not always result in the people getting their stolen money back. Even in those cases where some restitution was made, the legal fees for litigation would take away most of the recovery.

There are several good plans for avoiding probate, and each will be discussed. However, the plan that is so simple, easy and inexpensive—the one that lawyers do not seem to like—is the Revocable Living Trust.

In the beginning, the purposes of probate laws were to determine the validity of a will and to protect the estate until it could be distributed according to the directions of the testator or the applicable statutes. In the early days when estates normally consisted of land, and all the interested parties and the property were usually located in the same area, it is easy to see how each state had its own set of probate laws, frequently different from other states. There was little need in those days for uniformity. However, in modern times estates are often composed of paper assets—stocks, bonds, pension plans, insurance benefits, and vacation homes or condominiums in far off places. People are more mobile now, with potential heirs living in many different places.

The old probate laws are simply outdated, unrealistic, burdened with complexity, and administered by lawyers and judges who seem to be preoccupied with obfuscation and habit.

The Uniform Probate Code has made some progress in simplifying the procedures, but much remains to be done. The Uniform Probate Code eliminates the need for a lengthy and complicated settlement process when a will is not contested. This reduces legal fees, court costs, and delays. The code clarifies the status of *will substitutes*, such as jointly held property and bank accounts, and establishes a reasonable distribution of assets, mostly to the surviving spouse or other close family members, when there is no will.

The Uniform Probate Code has been adopted in part in only a few states over the vociferous objections of those individuals and organizations having vested interests in the old process.

The inefficiency of the probate system, the conspiracy of silence among the members of the legal community, the inability of the judicial system to make any significant improvements, and the frustration of the public has resulted in an avalanche of probate avoidance methods and techniques. The legal community, of course, continues to resist the concept that laymen can handle legal problems themselves. However, during the past few years there has been an exciting boom in the scramble to avoid probate. Along with this awareness of the public that they can avoid probate without the services of a lawyer has come the publication of a variety of legal guides and kits designed to tell people about these plans—and demonstrate how to use them, legally.

These methods are easy to understand, and very easy for laymen to use. It is simply a matter of getting accurate information and instructions.

The Revocable Living Trust, the most popular method for avoiding probate, is as easy to prepare as your own will. The Revocable Living Trust involves an agreement by which one party, the grantor, transfers property to a trustee to hold for the benefit of another, the beneficiary, and is created during the lifetime of the grantor, the person creating the trust.

Revocable means that the grantor retains the right to revoke the trust, change its terms, or regain possession of the trust property. An irrevocable living trust exists when the grantor relinquishes title to property placed in the trust and gives up all right to revoke, amend, alter, or terminate the trust.

One person can be grantor, trustee, and beneficiary. This principle of law is the basis upon which many people avoid all probate processes. Typically, a person can create a revocable trust in which he is cotrustee with another person, for example, an adult child or partner, to hold and manage the estate, and upon the death of the grantor there is no probate of the trust property. It is that simple.

This is an easy procedure, used by many people, which you can employ to completely avoid probate and still have complete control over all of your property. Here are the steps in the procedure:

- You execute a revocable living trust agreement in which you are cotrustee with another person.
- You can convey all, or any part, of your property.
- You provide for income for yourself during your lifetime.
- You provide that upon your death the property is to be distributed by the cotrustee as you direct in the trust agreement.

The main characteristics of this kind of arrangement are:

- You can cancel at any time during your life.
- You retain complete control of your assets.
- You can receive all benefits and income.
- There is no probate, no probate expenses, confusion, intimidation, or humiliation.
- Your beneficiaries can get their inheritance immediately.
- There are no public proceedings nor court records; your financial affairs are kept private and confidential.

When a person dies, he is no longer able to exercise dominion or control over the property he owned or controlled during his life. Through proper estate planning prior to death a person can direct and articulate with particularity what shall and shall not be done with his property.

If a person wants to dispose of property by will, as permitted under the law, the property must pass according to the terms of a valid will. If, on the other hand, a person does not have a will, the law, as set out in the statutes of each state, through the laws of descent and distribution, or intestate succession, provides for the transfer of the property to the persons designated in the statutes.

In either event—by will or by statutory law—the passing of property is accomplished by a court drama called probate proceedings, or the probate process.

Probate is a court procedure by which a will is proved to be valid or invalid. This generally includes all matters and proceedings under the probate statutes pertaining to the administration of estates, guardianships, and other personal and estate matters. These proceedings involve the appointment or designation of an executor, personal representative, or administrator, who under the supervision of the probate court, collects, manages, maintains, and distributes the assets of an estate after payment of claims, costs, court fees, and other probate expenses.

Our probate laws were originally formulated in England at a time in which there was very little mobility by most people and in which estates were largely composed of land or property affixed to land. The development of our probate laws in early American history also evolved at a time in which there was relatively little mobility in our society. However, in modern times, with a highly mobile society in which families typically reside in many different states, own various kinds of property in different states, and are frequently traveling to numerous locations, the probate laws have become out of touch with contemporary reality. They represent little more than an obstacle that must be overcome before an estate can be settled.

The probate process as it is practiced in America is a virtual cancer upon the legal community, and neither the shame of scandals, corruption, and excessive greed, nor the dictates of ethics, conscience, common decency, common sense, or duty to clients can motivate the lawyers and the legislators to improve it.

Unfortunately, modest estates or inheritances get caught up in the majestic web of the probate process, and these modest estates are usually much smaller or nonexistent by the time they escape from the jaws of the probate trap with its extravagant fees, unending delays, and probate costs.

What Law Governs?

The law of the place from which the executor or personal representative derives his authority, as it exists at the time of administration, governs the administration of estates. Thus, it is important in the preparation of a will or other estate planning program that you look to the laws of the state where a person lives or is domiciled and where property is located and will be probated after death.

Although the laws of each state might vary on some items, the adoption of the Uniform Probate Code has somewhat simplified the understanding of the probate laws by some American citizens. In the final analysis, the court that probates an estate will apply the laws of the state where the court is located, with rare exceptions.

What Is the Administration of an Estate?

The administration of an estate is the management of the decedent's estate for the purpose of collecting and preserving the assets, paying debts, and making distribution to those entitled to the property. A personal representative is the person who handles the administration of the estate. An executor is a personal representative appointed by a testator in a will. An administrator is a personal representative appointed by the court to act where there is no executor appointed by a will. Executors and administrators are considered to be officers of the court and they have a high fiduciary duty to the estate and to creditors and beneficiaries. Most are required to make an accounting to the court.

While executors are nominated by the decedent, an administrator is appointed by the court, and generally is a surviving spouse, next of kin, a creditor, a person having an interest in the estate, or a friend of the judge.

As a general rule, any person who is capable of writing a will is competent to act as executor or administrator. However, where management and supervision of assets is involved, the person should have experience in business activities. Some persons can be disqualified to serve as executors or administrators; for example, nonresidents (in some states) and judges of the probate court.

Generally, only a person who has an interest in an estate can apply for the administration of the estate. The order of preference here is also surviving spouse, next of kin, creditors or others having claims, or friends of the probate judge.

Personal representatives generally have the duties and responsibilities to:

- Discover assets of the decedent.
- Collect and preserve the assets.
- Maintain custody, control, and management of the estate, including the management of a going business, contracts, business transactions, if any, investments, tort claims, real estate, litigation, and the like until the estate is settled.
- Provide for an allowance to surviving spouse and children.
- Pay all claims, estate taxes, probate expenses, and other obligations.

- Distribute the balance to the beneficiaries.
- Make an accounting to the probate court and obtain an order of discharge.

An essential duty of the executor or administrator after appointment is to collect all assets of the decedent in order that they can be identified and administered. Not only is he responsible in this respect as to all the decedent's property he already knows about, but it is also his responsibility to discover the full extent of the decedent's assets. If he has reason to believe that any asset exists or might exist, even though his knowledge of it is incomplete, he is required to make all investigations necessary to learn the truth. One of his first duties, therefore, is to familiarize himself as fully as possible with the decedent's affairs.

All assets placed in a Revocable Living Trust by a decedent will be entirely exempt from this probate scenario.

Nature of Office of Executors and Administrators

Executors and administrators are not public officers within the commonly accepted meaning of that term, although they are regarded as officers of the court, and the positions they hold are frequently referred to as offices. Actually, the position is a trust. They are trustees, and funds of the estate in their hands are trust funds.

The executor represents the testator and it is part of his duty to see that the will of the testator is properly executed. The executor also represents the legatees for whose benefit probate proceedings are held. An administrator represents the heirs of the deceased in whose interest the law provides for the distribution of the estate by an administrator, but the administrator does not represent any particular heir.

A Trustee of a Revocable Living Trust accomplishes the same objective as probate administration, but without any probate court supervision or lawyer fees and court costs.

Purpose of Administration

The administration of estates involves more than merely interpreting wills and decreeing the evolution of property. It involves the collection of assets, particularly personal assets, and using them for the payment of debts, taxes, and costs of administration until all are paid or the assets exhausted. If, after full administration, a balance remains, the payment of the balance to those entitled to it is called distribution. It is most unfortunate, as previously noted, that some estates are exhausted by administration costs, legal fees, and other probate costs.

Necessity of Administration

Theoretically, administration of a decedent's estate is necessary in all cases, because the title to the personal property does not descend to the next of kin, and without administration there would be no legal authority to represent the estate in litigation or collect assets and pay debts, taxes, and other costs. However, there are instances in some states where persons entitled to an estate have been permitted to take possession of property without the necessity of administration, when nothing remained for a final disposition of the estate except distribution of the property. In fact, the Uniform Probate Code, as originally drafted, encourages simplicity of distribution where there are no disputes.

Of course, there is no necessity for the administration of an estate where the owner elects to avoid probate by one of the plans discussed in later chapters.

Appointment, Qualifications, and Tenure of Executors and Administrators

A court makes no initial appointment of an executor; its power is generally limited to recognizing and approving or disapproving an appointment made by the testator. A court will generally carry out the intention of the testator by appointing the executor designated by the testator.

The fact that an executor derives his authority primarily from a will serves to distinguish him from an administrator who is appointed by a probate court from a person or class designated by statute and who derives his power solely from his appointment by the court.

Bonds and/or Good Faith Required

Administration bonds are required to protect creditors and next of kin from loss through the default or fraud of the personal representative. The bonds constitute a means of indemnity to the estate; the bond fees are paid out of the estate.

An executor or administrator has a duty to exercise the utmost good faith in all his transactions affecting the estate. He cannot advance his own personal interest at the expense of the heirs, and any fraud by the executor or administrator will justify the court in declaring his acts void. This is the law, but in many probate courts the participants sing a different song.

In the performance of his fiduciary duties, an executor or an administrator must exercise the diligence that an ordinarily prudent person would exercise under like circumstances in his own affairs. He is not an insurer or a guarantor, but he must use ordinary care, prudence, skill, and diligence.

A personal representative can be held liable for losses to the estate resulting from his or her failure to exercise the diligence expected of a prudent and cautious person or from a failure to use common skill and ordinary business caution.

Phases of Estate Administration

In many respects a legal representative steps into the shoes of the decedent and takes his place in all matters having to do with the decedent's property rights and financial obligations. Frequently this involves the executor in nonfinancial matters, including personal relations of the decedent or among the beneficiaries—any of the problems and situations that can confront an individual during lifetime. The possible range of these problems is unlimited.

Estate administration might necessitate involvement in any field of human activity. It can involve problems of personalities and all kinds of other human problems. It can open closet doors to expose family secrets that during life the decedent had carefully concealed. It also affords a cross section of life, of business, of law, of economics, of human vanity and nobility.

On the other hand, the administration of an estate offers constructive opportunities to minimize taxes and expenses, to preserve assets, and protect and enhance the security of beneficiaries. The responsibility of a legal representative is great, which emphasizes the care that should be taken by a testator in selecting one. An executor and his risks are correspondingly great, and one should not accept the appointment without realizing the potential personal liabilities involved.

The Uniform Probate Code

As previously suggested, the Uniform Probate Code was intended to provide ways in which the time for probate proceedings could be substantially shortened, the procedures simplified, and the legal fees, court costs, and expenses lessened. The code is a very flexible document. In difficult or controversial estates, it permits all of the formalities that the laws of most states afford. However, in routine, noncontroversial estates, it provides a process for speedy handling and relatively inexpensive settlement and distribution of an estate. There are also avenues that permit lawyers and personal representatives to adopt a middle ground—by taking great precaution in certain matters, but opting for simplicity and speed in others.

The objectives of the system are to provide necessary opportunities and safeguards to permit persons interested in decedents' estates to be able to settle estates with quite minimal contact with the public office. It is inherent in the approach, however, that interested persons, including personal representatives, are enabled to use the court system for binding all interested persons by order following a mailed notice and a hearing. They can secure a final order on any matter that might involve an estate or a personal representative. The key concept is that the court or registrar does not exercise supervisory jurisdiction over its appointees. The court has no authority to check the work of a personal representative or to make orders relating to him, except when either the representative or other interested persons petition for some order or relief in proceedings begun after the appointment has been completed.

Informal Proceedings

Informal proceedings are defined in the code as those conducted without notice to interested persons by an officer of the court acting as a registrar or judge for probate of a will or appointment of a personal representative.

Under the code, if a decedent leaves a valid will it can be informally probated without the appointment of an executor or other personal representative. Assuming no survivor initiates a formal testacy proceeding, those interested in a decedent's will, or as heirs of a person with no will, can take advantage of the informal proceedings without a formal adjudication process.

Priority for Appointment as Personal Representative

Persons who are not disqualified have priority for appointment as personal representatives in the following order:

- The person with priority as determined by a probated will including a person nominated by a power conferred in a will.
- The surviving spouse of a decedent who is a devisee of the decedent.
- Other devisees of the decedent.
- The surviving spouse of the decedent (without being specified as a devisee).
- Other heirs of the decedent.
- Any creditor, 45 days after the death of the decedent.

Application for Informal Probate Proceedings

Under the code, an informal probate or appointment proceeding is initiated by filling an application as described in the statutes.

Applications for informal appointment are directed to the registrar or judge, and verified by the applicant to be accurate and complete to the best of his knowledge and belief as to the information required. Most courts have printed forms for your use.

Duties and Responsibilities of Executor, Administrator, or Other Person Interested in the Estate of a Decedent

One of the most elusive things about the probate process that most people who have an interest in the probate of estates do not realize is that most of the work involved in the so-called probate of an estate is not legal work. A lawyer is not required to do it. If you can follow the checklist that follows, you can save a great deal of time, money, and frustration simply by knowing what is to be done, who should do it, and how to keep control over the activities of your lawyer rather than just turning it all over to the lawyer. It is simply a myth that all probate matters involve legal work that must be done by lawyers.

Everything you do will save on legal fees, and knowing what should and should not be done by lawyers will also result in great savings for the estate. Your understanding of the procedures will enable you to avoid a lot of the unnecessary work that most probate lawyers routinely do to increase their fees.

Review these step-by-step procedures and do your own research to do your job efficiently, effectively, and competently, and require the same from your lawyer.

Before Probate Proceedings

Most, if not all, of the work to be done before the actual probate proceedings can, and should, be done by the executor or administrator. Lawyers are not normally required and should not be involved in these preliminaries.

Notice of Decease

Give notice to all banks, savings and loan associations, credit unions, brokerage accounts, financial institutions, and other businesses where the decedent has accounts or business relationships. Obtain passbooks, certificates, factual data, and all other information about the accounts. It might also be appropriate, depending on the family situation, to give notices to family friends and business associates. Later, if the probate proceedings are instituted, a formal notice might be required to be published.

Insurance

Check insurance coverage on all of the decedent's estate, including property, casualty, and life insurance. It will be necessary to determine all coverage for the purposes of protecting assets, changing insurance coverage as appropriate, and in assisting in making claims on life coverage.

It might be appropriate in some situations to change the name of the insured from the decedent's name to the estate. In other situations, where title to property passes on to the beneficiaries, it might be appropriate to wait and transfer the insurance coverage along with title to the property.

Although life insurance is generally payable directly to the beneficiaries, it might be appropriate for an executor to assist the beneficiaries in the settlement of insurance claims. If life insurance proceeds are a part of the estate for tax purposes, it might be necessary for an executor to make proper tax returns.

Mail

Notify the post office and arrange for receipt of decedent's mail. It is also generally appropriate when you notify friends and business associates to request that mail be addressed directly to you instead of the decedent.

Copy of Will, If Any

Make additional copies of the decedent's will, if any, for beneficiaries, taxing authorities, and others who need it. You will be surprised to learn how many people have some interest or claim in estates and want a copy of the will. You also will be surprised at the number of people who show great surprise at being left out of a will. Of course, one can get a copy of the will from the probate court, but it is much easier, less expensive, much less trouble, and saves time to have extra copies available.

Copies of Death Certificate

Make several copies of the death certificate because it will be needed in many of the transactions in connection with the collection of the property, and the management and distribution of the estate. Extra copies will be needed for social security, insurance claims, bank transactions, and many other items.

Family Conference

Schedule a family conference at which all interested parties can be advised of the facts available and exchange information and ideas about the handling of the estate.

This could be one of the most important single things you will do in the administration of an estate. The more you know about what has to be done and who should do it, the more you will gain the confidence of the beneficiaries, family members, and others who are interested in the estate. This emphasizes the importance of your learning about the probate process before you are thrust into the role of executor or administrator.

There are a number of subjects that should be discussed at these meetings. Discretion is required as to how many meetings to hold, who attends, what is discussed, and what is done. If you handle it in an efficient manner by being prepared with a checklist or agenda of things to be done, and suggestions as to who should do it, you will not only gain the confidence of all those involved, but you can save a lot of potential conflicts and friction among family members.

Determine in advance of this meeting what topics should be avoided, what can be accomplished, and how it can be accomplished.

One of the most critical things to take care of is the immediate needs of the surviving spouse and close family members.

Burial Arrangements

Social security or veterans benefits are sometimes involved in making burial arrangements. Rarely will an executor be appointed by the court before the funeral. Therefore, it is generally some member of the family that will assist in making burial arrangements, sometimes under great stress and intimidation. Proper estate planning by the decedent can greatly facilitate what can otherwise be a very complex and expensive ordeal.

Consider Employment of Attorney

The family conference is a good time to discuss the need for the employment of an attorney, and, if so, who. Where a decedent has a regular attorney who assisted in the estate planning, the choice can be easy. However, in a vast majority of the cases, the decedent not only did not have an attorney, but most likely did not have any significant estate plans or other activities calculated to make the administration of the estate any easier.

You might have to delay a decision as to whether a lawyer is needed. Don't make the mistake that many people make by automatically assuming that a lawyer is required. You must first learn enough about the estate to determine the need for a lawyer.

I have seen many situations where a surviving family would go to an attorney and hire him to probate an estate only to learn later that probate was unnecessary. This is not only expensive and awkward—it can be embarrassing for the attorney and for those who hire him. However, if there are any assets, most lawyers will plunge right in whether they are needed or not.

Safe Deposit Boxes, If Any

List the contents of any safety deposit boxes in decedent's name. Usually most state laws provide that certain persons must be present, including tax authorities, and that an inventory be made of all contents of safety deposit boxes. If you have a box in the joint name of yourself and another person it might not be necessary for the joint owner to have tax authorities hovering around when the box is opened, though some states now require that.

You should then take possession of all valuables and make sure they are properly protected and distributed.

Preliminary Estimate of Estate Property

Make a preliminary estimate of decedent's estate to determine what form the probate and administration of the estate will require. This is the point at which it might first become evident that the estate is so small as to come within the "no probate" provisions of the statutes. This is one of the items you will have researched as soon as you get a copy of your state statute.

Collection and Protection of Property

Search the household, make an inventory of all personal property, and arrange for storage and protection of personal property. Discretion is required where there is a surviving spouse who is living in the home. In fact, you might have very little to do with personal tangible property in this situation. Don't interfere where you are not required by law to do so. Moreover, most decedents and their survivors do not want unnecessary "poking around" by lawyers or executors where they are not necessary.

Real estate protection and management is of particular importance where the decedent owned apartments, business buildings, or other real estate that needs day to day management. A going business usually requires immediate attention unless there is a surviving partner or manager.

The title to automobiles in the decedent's name can be especially troublesome. For example, family members will usually want to drive an automobile, but the estate might be liable for any accident in which the automobile is involved. Make sure all cars have proper insurance coverage and either sell the cars for cash or transfer the title to beneficiaries as soon as possible.

The decedent's checkbook and bank records can be the greatest source of information about the financial transactions in which the decedent was involved. Moreover, they will be essential for later use in preparing tax returns.

All cash owned by decedent should be accounted for, put to work, used for estate obligations, or distributed to the persons who are entitled to receive it.

If the living facilities of a decedent should become vacant it is essential to avoid losses and damages by failure to properly protect and manage the property. Where business property is not being managed by a surviving spouse or partner, it is important to take quick action in disposing of the property or obtaining competent management. Make sure there is adequate insurance coverage on all property.

Transfer title, if appropriate, to personal property. If the estate is uncomplicated, and the probate is not delayed, you will probably wish to transfer title to most personal property directly to the beneficiaries. However, if you anticipate delays, complex or extended litigation, tax claims, or other conflicts that will require long probate processes, you might wish to transfer title to income producing property to the estate. This is a matter of discretion and will depend on the facts in each case. In all events, be alert to the problems involved and be prepared to solve them without unnecessary confusion or delay.

Collect any rents, interest, dividends, royalties, or debts due to the estate. Until you can complete the administration of an estate it will be your duty to take care of all financial transactions involving the assets of the estate. You might be required to institute legal action to collect some of the debts owed to the decedent or to the estate.

Assemble data on all property owned by the decedent that will not be a part of the probate estate. Jointly owned property, trust property, life insurance proceeds, and other assets might be a part of the taxable estate—for tax purposes only—but pass directly to others without any probate proceedings. Where tax problems occur it will be part of your duty to make tax returns revealing all the facts, including the value and aggregate amounts.

In appropriate cases, it might be necessary to have appraisers appointed in the sale or disposition of some of the assets. Don't assume all appraisers are competent or honest. Carefully review the qualifications of any appraiser appointed, and be sure you have a fee arrangement in writing. Moreover, you might want to take a look at old probate files and be sure you do not hire an appraiser who is a "buddy" of the probate judge and the probate lawyers.

Utilities, Charge Accounts, and Credit Cards

There are a number of business activities of a decedent that should be closed down as soon as possible. Credit cards, unless being used by the surviving spouse or jointly held by descendant or next of kin, should be collected and cancelled. You might want to transfer some accounts into the name of the estate, for example, utilities, telephone, and other services that are needed by you, the family, or business. Otherwise it is appropriate to close out the accounts of a decedent or have them transferred to the surviving spouse or other family members.

Employer Benefits

Many of the decedent's personal matters can be handled by the surviving spouse or other family members. However, it is usually appropriate and proper for an executor to assist in the matters of salary, bonuses, and any distributions from pension or profit sharing plans.

Open Estate Bank Accounts

If the probate is complicated, or, for other reasons, might last a long time, you probably will need a bank account in the name of the estate. This will facilitate your being able to carry on the financial transactions necessary to bring the estate to a close. Generally this will not occur until after probate proceedings are filed and you are officially appointed.

Personal Records and Tax Returns

Assemble all personal records and tax returns of the decedent to bring yourself current on all the financial transactions of the decedent. These records will be essential for obtaining the background information and facts you will need to handle the estate properly, and to prepare tax returns.

Social Security, Civil Service, Veterans, and Other Benefits

These benefits are also items that might be more of a personal problem for the surviving members of the family. However, the filing of required paperwork is frequently handled by an executor. An attorney will charge high fees for this nonlegal work that any layman could do.

Family Allowance and Assistance

Each state statute has a provision for family allowances pending probate of an estate. You can get preliminary information on these items at the first family conference.

Going Business

Obtain all information about any partnership agreements, buy–sell agreements, or other business arrangements of the decedent.

Check any litigation, claims, or other controversies relating to the decedent's property or property interests. In the case of a going business, quick action is needed to manage the business yourself or obtain competent management personnel.

Current Bills and Obligations

Formulate some estimates early in the probate process as to whether the estate is solvent or potentially insolvent. If you are sure the estate is solvent you might wish to pay current bills and obligations to avoid interest and penalties. However, if questions remain as to whether the estate is solvent, be cautious about making any payments on estate obligations. In most situations it might be appropriate to require a claimant to file a claim in the probate proceedings. Telephone and utility bills might have to be paid to avoid termination of services.

Do You Need a Lawyer?

After holding the family conference and completing the preliminary estimate of the estate's assets, you will be in a position to know whether an attorney should be employed to assist in probate court. If no probate is necessary, you can generally forget about hiring a lawyer. Furthermore, in situations where most of the property was jointly owned and there are no tax problems or possibilities of litigation, there is no need for a lawyer. You will be surprised to learn how much you can do yourself by reviewing the statutes and court rules with the intention of doing all of the things you are permitted to do as executor or administrator.

Determining That Probate Is Unnecessary

Your preliminary estimate of assets and your initial review of your state's statutes will enable you to make this determination, usually without the need for a lawyer's advice. In a vast majority of cases a lawyer is not required. Moreover, unless some conflict or controversy arises, there is virtually nothing for a lawyer to do in a small estate—other than doing the executor's work and getting paid legal fees for it.

Probate Proceedings Step by Step

If probate is deemed necessary, because of contesting of the will, estate tax problems, size of the estate, or any other legal reason, follow the steps outlined in the following sections.

Preliminary Information

First, determine the domicile of the decedent for probate purposes, the place of administration and the possibility of ancillary probate in other states. Avoid probate in other states when possible. Then determine whether formal or informal probate is appropriate. Keep this question in mind when you first review your state's statutes.

Initial Proceedings in Court

Offer the will for probate or apply for administration. Obtain Letters Testamentary or Letters of Administration and make extra copies of these documents for banks, claims, and other transactions. If bonds are required, make arrangements for them. Complete the publication of any notice required by statutes or rules to interested parties and creditors. Arrange for ancillary administration, if necessary. Prepare and file a complete inventory of the decedent's assets with the probate court.

Tax Aspects of Estate Administration

Although you might need an accountant to assist in the preparation of tax returns, become familiar with all the necessary forms and the instructions for completing them. These can be obtained from IRS offices. Get a copy of IRS Publication 559, Federal Tax Guide for Survivors, Executors, and Administrators, and other information on tax requirements for an estate.

Some of the usual requirements that you might have to know about include the following:

- Apply for a tax identification number.
- File Income Tax Return, Form 1040 for decedent.
- File Form 712, Life Insurance Statement.
- File Fiduciary Income Tax Return, Form 1041.
- File Estate Tax Return, Form 706.
- File U.S. Quarterly Gift Tax Return, Form 709.

Claims Against the Estate

Legitimate claims should be paid as soon as reasonably possible to avoid interest and penalties, provided the estate is solvent and has funds available. Investigate all estate claims to make sure they are valid. In the event litigation should develop, your lawyer can handle it for you, but you can assist by having available all facts, evidence, and witnesses.

Distribution of Estate

Once you are permitted by the court to actually distribute the assets, you should do so in the following order:

- Pay all taxes due.
- Pay all expenses, fees, and other administration costs of probate.
- Satisfy all claims against the estate.

- Pay family allowances.
- Satisfy specific bequests.
- Satisfy general bequests.
- Make residuary distribution.

Accounting

Keep records of all transactions so you can account to beneficiaries, tax authorities, and the court. You will need a final accounting of all assets for these and other purposes.

Order of Discharge

After completion of all acts necessary to conclude the probate proceedings, file your application for an order of discharge. It is at an end.

Chapter 10

The Revocable
Living Trust

A trust is a legal relationship in which one person transfers property to a second person for the benefit of a third person. The person creating the trust is called the grantor, trustor, or settler. The person or entity having legal title to the trust property is the trustee, and the person for whose benefit the trust is created is called the beneficiary. The same person can be grantor, trustee, and beneficiary all at the same time in some situations.

The fundamental legal principle you need to understand about a trust is that one person can have two legal entities: as an individual, and as a trustee. For legal, tax, and other purposes a trustee is a separate person or entity from the person as an individual. Therefore, an individual person can transfer property from his or her individual name to himself or herself *as trustee*, and hold it for himself or for others. Typically, the Revocable Living Trust Agreement provides that title shall be in the name of the trustee or cotrustees and upon the death of the grantor shall go to the designated beneficiary or beneficiaries. When the grantor dies the property is automatically held by the cotrustee or successor trustee for the beneficiaries without any probate process or court proceedings. This might sound like a bit of legal magic, and, indeed,that is exactly what it is: it is an accepted legal fiction to accomplish a noble and worthwhile goal. It avoids probate just as slick as "magic."

Elements of a Trust

The essential elements of a trust are: intention, trust property, trustee, and beneficiary. It is necessary for you to understand the importance of these terms in order for you to create your own trust.

Intention

A trust is created only if the grantor properly expresses an intention to create a trust. Generally, a trust can be created by written instrument, verbally, or by conduct. The Statute of Frauds and Statute of Wills requires that some transactions must be in writing to be enforceable. When the transaction is only oral, the evidence is required to be clear and convincing. No particular form of written wording or conduct is necessary. Even though many oral agreements are legal it is recommended that you always manifest your intentions by a written document, especially in the case of a trust agreement.

Trust Property

A trust cannot be created unless there is trust property that definitely exists. Any transferable interest, present or future, vested or contingent, legal or equitable, in any object of ownership, tangible or intangible, can be held in trust. This would include virtually any kind of property you own.

Trustee

A trust by its very nature requires that there be a trustee to administer it. However, if you place property in a trust without naming a trustee, or the trustee dies, a court would appoint a trustee to administer the trust. Be specific in naming a trustee and successor trustees to avoid the unnecessary costs of a court appointment.

As a general rule, any natural person, including the grantor, can hold property in trust in the same way that a person can hold property for his or her own benefit. Moreover, other entities can act as trustees, such as a bank, trust company, or corporation. Where a major objective of a trust is to avoid probate and the excessive fees associated with probate system you might wish to avoid naming an attorney, a bank or trust company because the fees they charge are an integral part of the probate system.

A property owner can declare himself trustee of the property for the benefit of another. In this situation the property owner is both grantor and trustee. The selection of a trustee other than yourself can be one of the most important aspects of creating a trust. Most people select a close family member, friend, or relative. Under the typical Revocable Living Trust Agreement the only duty of a successor trustee is to convey the trust property to the beneficiaries. If management of a business or other investments are involved, consider a person with business experience.

Beneficiary

A private trust, unlike charitable or honorary trusts, requires a beneficiary with the right to enforce it. The beneficiary either must be specifically named or be reasonably ascertained from facts existing at the time the trust is created.

Any person, natural or corporate, who has the capacity to take and hold title to property can be beneficiary even though that person might not be capable of administering the property. Indeed, the inability of a beneficiary to manage his own property, as in the case of minor children, is often a principal reason for creating a trust.

There can be any number of beneficiaries, and the grantor can be the only beneficiary, or one of several. The trustee can also be a beneficiary with one exception: a sole trustee cannot be a sole beneficiary.

Methods of Creating a Trust

You can create a trust:

- by declaring that you hold your property as trustee for yourself and/or others
- by transferring your property to another person as trustee for yourself and/or others
- by transferring, in your will, your property to another person as trustee for others

Creating a trust by will is called a testamentary trust that must go through the probate system. Always use a formal written document when creating a trust to avoid any confusion or misunderstanding, and do not use the testamentary trust if you wish to avoid probate.

Many people have come to consider the revocable living trust as an instrument that incorporates most of the features of a will. It not only accomplishes the objectives of a will more efficiently, less expensively, and in less time, but it has a host of other advantages.

The Revocable Living Trust

The most popular trust, by far, is the revocable living trust. Its use as a technique for avoiding probate has become very popular during the past few years, and it is anticipated that it will continue its dramatic increase in popularity with the general public.

A revocable living trust is an arrangement in which an individual places property in trust, naming himself or some other person as trustee or cotrustee, but reserving the right to revoke the trust so that the property can be returned to the grantor. Generally the trust agreement provides that upon the death of the grantor the property shall go to the named beneficiaries. This automatically avoids all probate of the property. A revocable living trust also can be used to place income producing property in trust to be managed by professional managers. However, the grantor can actively manage the trust property if it is appropriate at any time. The primary purpose is the avoidance of the ineffective, inefficient, cumbersome, and expensive probate system.

The use of revocable living trust avoids the delays that are always involved in the probate courts, and prevents disruption that can occur where management of assets shifts after death. A trustee can distribute the assets of the estate immediately after death and needs no lawyers, judges, or other legal experts who are preoccupied with make-work paper shuffling to prolong the process. Another advantage is that a revocable living trust preserves the grantor's right of privacy while probate proceedings are a matter of public record.

Advantages of a Revocable Living Trust

In the typical revocable living trust, a grantor transfers property to a trustee under a written agreement. The classic arrangement is for the agreement to provide for the trustee to pay the grantor all of the income from the trust during his lifetime, together with such amounts of principal as might be requested by the grantor. It also provides that the grantor can amend or revoke the trust or change the trustee at any time.

Upon the death of the grantor the trust property is held, administered, and distributed by the trustee or successor trustee instead of passing under a will through the probate system. This method is fast, simple, easy, all without the costs and delays of probate. Indeed, it has been said that with a revocable living trust an estate can be completely administered before a lawyer can get to the courthouse to file a will! And it is true. An entire estate can be administered and distributed in a matter of a few hours or days. The express provisions of the trust agreement that apply to the administration and distribution of the trust assets after the death of the grantor become operative and can be carried out immediately.

The revocable living trust is the answer to most of the ugly probate problems. The trustee can perform all of the necessary management of the trust assets, if needed, including the collection of income, the purchase and sale of trust assets, and the management of a closely held business or real estate. In an emergency the trustee can make payment of hospital, nursing and doctor bills, and any other expenses of the grantor. The trust can be revoked by the grantor if he so desires, or the grantor can actively manage the trust property while leaving the legal title in the name of the trustee. If the grantor dies, the trust property can be immediately transferred to the designated beneficiaries. To summarize, the advantages of the revocable living trust include the following:

- Avoiding probate
- Avoiding probate administration fees and expenses
- Avoiding excessive legal fees for probate
- Avoiding unnecessary delays

- Avoiding publicity of probate matters
- Avoiding ancillary administration
- Avoiding statutory restrictions on bequests of property
- Avoiding inheritance taxes
- Avoiding will contests
- Saving taxes in some situations
- Managing property
- Avoiding interrupted management by incapacity of grantor
- Avoiding interrupted income and access to principal for family beneficiaries
- Avoiding the emotional trauma, aggravation, and frustration of a complicated probate process that does not serve any noble purpose.

Trusts and Taxes

As a general rule, a trust, like an individual, is a taxable entity. A trustee must file an income tax return for the trust and pay the tax on its taxable income unless income is passed through to the beneficiaries—which is usually the case. Many times a trust is established primarily because the beneficiary is in a lower tax bracket than the grantor. The establishment of several trusts can result in income tax savings on a grand scale in some circumstances. Although trusts can avoid probate they do not avoid estate or gift taxes as a general rule. Other techniques are recommended for avoiding estate and gift taxes.

Marital Property Rights

In most states the laws give certain legal rights to a surviving spouse that cannot be defeated by will. Some of these state laws, but not all, also give certain rights to a surviving spouse that cannot be defeated by gifts, by the revocable living trust or other transfers. These marital property rights are called community property, dower, curtesy, elective rights, statutory rights, or various other terms. These rights typically gives one-half or one-third, or some other portion of the estate of the decedent to the surviving spouse.

If community property is to be placed in a revocable trust by a married person, the grantor's spouse should join in the execution of the trust agreement. In general community property consists of whatever property is gained during the marriage by the toil, talent, or other productive faculty of either spouse. In general, property obtained by one spouse by gift, devise, or descent is not included in community property. In community property states, check the specific laws of your state on this question. The community property states are Arizona, California, Idaho, Louisiana, New Mexico, Nevada, Texas, and Washington. Some of the other states also give certain marital property rights to spouses, and these vary from state to state. Therefore, it is suggested that all transfers of property by a married person be signed by the spouse of the grantor. This is not a problem for most married people as they generally own property in joint names.

The concept behind these laws is that with certain exceptions, property acquired during marriage belongs to both spouses. The marital property rights vary from state to state and the state laws with respect to marital property rights transferred by a living trust agreement are inconsistent and sometimes difficult to interpret. It is recommended that any married person obtain the consent of the spouse in any trust created during marriage.

The trust doctrine was not fashioned by the courts as an instrument for denying rights of a spouse. On the contrary, the trust can be used by both married and unmarried persons as an easy, simple, inexpensive way to transfer property from one generation to another without the probate process.

Examples of How the Revocable Living Trust Works

Suppose that a married couple provides in a Revocable Living Trust Agreement that all, or a part of, their assets are declared to be held by them, as cotrustees, for their benefit during their lifetimes, and upon the death of either spouse to go to the surviving spouse, or in the event of simultaneous deaths to go directly to designated beneficiaries. Immediately upon the death of either spouse, all legal interests in all the property would automatically revert to the surviving spouse, as sole trustee, free and clear from any probate processes or other court delays. Upon the death of the surviving spouse the property would go to the successor trustee for the designated beneficiaries, free and clear from any probate processes or other court delays. The surviving spouse would have the option to place the assets in another Revocable Living Trust with an adult child or other family member as cotrustee and avoid probate again and again.

Suppose further, as a second example, that an unmarried person provides in a Revocable Living Trust Agreement that all, or a part of, his assets are declared to be held by the grantor and a third party, as cotrustees, for the grantor's benefit during his or her lifetime, and upon the death of the grantor to go to the beneficiaries designated in the agreement. Immediately upon the grantor's death, all legal interest in all the property would automatically revert to the cotrustee, as the sole trustee, to be transferred as directed by the grantor in the agreement. If the beneficiary is an adult he could be the cotrustee and upon the grantor's death he or she would automatically have title to the property for himself.

Trusts Take Precedence over a Will!

We have been discussing the two principle ways for you to pass your property upon your death to the persons you want to have it either by will or by a trust. The transfer by will requires the probate process; a Revocable Living Trust completely avoids probate.

What happens if you do both—leave property to a person in your will and also leave the same property to another person in a Revocable Living Trust? The trust takes precedence over the will. For example, if you have $100,000 in stocks and first write a valid will leaving the specific stocks to John Doe, and then later execute a Revocable Living Trust leaving the same stocks to Jane Doe, Jane Doe receives the stocks upon your death because the trust takes precedence. Suppose further that you first placed stocks in a Revocable Living Trust for John Doe and later executed a valid will leaving the same stocks to Jane Doe. In this case, John Doe receives the stocks. The trust takes precedence over the will no matter whether it was executed before or after the will.

The Revocable Living Trust takes precedence over the will in both cases because the title (ownership) of the property was transferred in each transaction when the trust agreement was executed. The title (ownership) to the stocks could not be transferred by will until the death of the owner. Even though you can revoke a trust and you can revoke a will the trust actually transfers title to the trustee at the time of the execution of the trust and a will does not.

Transferring Title to Property

In transferring title to property from a grantor to a trustee, the execution of the trust agreement and listing of the property in the Exhibit "A" schedule of property is legally sufficient for most property. However, there are various laws and regulations controlling the keeping of records for transfer of some property, and these should be followed to assure that your records are accurate and complete.

Records and Recording Laws

A public record is defined as one required by law to be kept, or necessary to be kept, in the discharge of a duty imposed by law, or directed by law to serve as a memorial and evidence of something written, said, or done. A public record is one made by a public officer in pursuance of a duty, the immediate purpose of which is to disseminate information to the public or to serve as a memorial of official transactions for public reference.

The system of recording is regulated by statute in each state. The recording requirements vary from state to state. However, every state has a statutory requirement for recording of conveyances or transfers of real estate. These records are usually kept at a county seat by a clerk or recorder. The typical statute requires the recording of all conveyances of real property, deeds, mortgages, deeds of trust or instruments in the nature of mortgages, and might include long term leases, chattel mortgages, mining claims, conveyances on execution, and other matters affecting real property.

The term *conveyance* has been defined as some written paper or instrument signed and delivered by one person to another, transferring the title to or creating a lien on property, or giving a right to a debt or duty.

Real Property

If any real property is included in the list of property in Exhibit "A," have the trust agreement acknowledged. It is also necessary to have a separate deed executed, transferring the property to the name of the trustee and then have the deed and the trust agreement recorded in the county where the real property is located. This is to comply with the recording statutes of the state. Obtain a real estate deed in your own state because they vary from state to state. These documents are available at local real estate offices, law offices, stationery stores, and other convenient places. Because you must record the real property trust, you might want to have separate trusts, one for real property, and another for all other property. This will enable you to record only the real property trust and keep the other matters private in a separate document. It is not necessary or appropriate to record a trust with personal property as trust property.

Personal Property

Stocks, bonds, mutual funds, bank accounts, saving and loan accounts, and other similar types of accounts can be included in your trust agreement. However, you need to check with the bank or other financial institution involved to make appropriate changes in their records and certificates of title, if any.

Automobiles, motorcycles, trailers, and similar kinds of property generally have a certificate of title that is recorded with the appropriate governmental agency.

The trustee's name is generally entered on these documents as, for example: "John Doe, as Trustee under Revocable Living Trust Agreement dated June 1, 1990." It is frequently abbreviated as follows: "John Doe, as Trustee u/t/d June 1, 1990."

Some of the financial institutions, especially banks, might want a copy of the trust agreement in their files. Check with these institutions and give them directions to make sure your trust agreements will be recognized.

In the event you have occasion to transfer additional property to the trust after it has been established or withdraw assets from it you simply add the new property to Exhibit "A" and date and sign it or delete property and date and sign it. Remember, you reserved the right in the instrument to amend or revoke it at any time.

If any property is jointly owned both owners will, of course, have to sign the trust agreement as grantors and also execute any deed or certificate of title.

Selection of Trustees and Successor Trustees

For purposes of avoiding probate, it is generally recommended that the grantor act as trustee or cotrustee. The grantor should consider a cotrustee especially if an adult beneficiary (for example, spouse or adult child) is a primary or sole beneficiary. A grantor who wants a third party trustee should consider adult children, other relatives, or business associates. Having a lawyer, trust officer, bank, or trust company as trustee defeats one of the major objectives of the trust: avoiding excessive fees and expenses of probate. It is also very important to appoint successor trustees because this avoids the expenses, delays, and inconvenience of court appointments.

Revocation and Amendment

The great advantage of the Revocable Living Trust is your ability, at any time, for any reason, or for no reason, to change it or revoke it. You can do this by the mere stroke of your pen. By using the revocation form you simply describe the trust agreement you wish to revoke and sign the revocation. If the trust agreement is recorded you need to record the revocation. Immediately upon your signing the revocation and transmitting it to the trustee, the trust is automatically terminated and revoked as a matter of law. No lawyers, no judges, or lengthy court proceedings are needed. You are in complete control of your property and it can remain a private matter, since you can keep it out of the hands of the probate lawyers.

This is necessarily a brief treatment of trusts, but the information given here and the forms that follow are entirely adequate for you to avoid probate. You have an absolute right to use a trust and to avoid probate and it is absolutely legal and valid in all states.

Revocable Living Trust Agreement Forms

The essence of avoiding probate via the Revocable Living Trust is simply to transfer title to property to a trustee by a written document. You, the grantor, can maintain complete control, management, and authority over the property. You can revoke at any time if you wish. In other words, the only difference is that you, or another, holds the *legal title* to the property, as trustee, and in the event of death the title to the property automatically—as a matter of law—is held as directed in the trust agreement to be used, or transferred, to the beneficiary or beneficiaries you have designated in the agreement. Thus, the probate of the assets, or transfer through the probate system, is avoided.

The Revocable Living Trust Agreement need not be complicated, complex, or mysterious. Each of the provisions of the typical trust are discussed here to demonstrate how simple it is and how you can do it yourself.

Whereas Clause

After preparing the introductory clause that merely states the names and identities of the grantor or grantors and the trustee or trustees, the so-called *Whereas Clause* simply states the grantor's intent, which is an essential element of a trust. It identifies the property and states the purpose of the agreement, the use and disposition of the property.

Transfer of Property

The transfer, or conveyance, of the property is the key to avoiding probate. Since the property is transferred to a trustee the grantor does not own it as a part of his estate to be disposed of in a will.

Disposition of Income and Principal

You have a legal right to direct exactly what is to happen with the property during your lifetime and after death. You can direct that all such property and all income therefrom shall be used by you or anyone else you designate. In the event any beneficiary is a minor you can direct the trustee to hold the property until the minor reaches majority.

Revocation and Amendment

You have a legal right to cancel the agreement at any time or change it in any way you desire.

Successor Trustee

It is important to have a trustee, a cotrustee, or successor trustee, to hold the title after the death of the grantor. This avoids the necessity for a court appointment—a potentially expensive venture into the domain of the probate system.

Trustee's Acceptance

Because this is an agreement, the other party, the trustee, must agree to the terms of the agreement and sign it.

Signatures

All grantors and all trustees must sign the agreement. Review the discussion about recording the documents in the event of real estate requirements for recording conveyance documents so you can be assured that the transfer meets all the legal requirements of your state's recording laws.

Exhibit "A" Schedule of Property

This is the place for listing and specifically identifying the property that is the subject of the trust. Make sure you use the legal description of real estate to avoid any doubts about the transfer of title on the record.

There are other provisions you can use in the agreements, but these are the essential parts for avoiding probate.

If you have any difficulty in completing the trust agreements, you might want to obtain a do it yourself kit with fill in forms. Whether you prepare your own forms from the following samples or use a kit, the following information will assist you in correctly filling in the blanks.

Notes on Using the Forms

Form 16 is for use by a married couple only, while the other forms are suitable for any adult. Married persons should consider carefully the marital rights of surviving spouses.

In each form the introductory paragraph should be filled in by listing the complete names and addresses of the grantor or grantors, and the trustee or cotrustees. The following example illustrates this first paragraph.

"This Revocable Living Trust Agreement is made this 15th day of June, 1990, between John J. Doe, and Jane J. Doe, husband and wife, of 123 Main Street, Boulder, Colorado, 80301, herein referred to as Grantors, and John J. Doe and Jane J. Doe, of 123 Main Street, Boulder, Colorado, 80301, herein referred to as cotrustees."

Paragraph 2 provides that the trust estate and income shall be used by the grantor or grantors during their lives, and upon the death of the grantor or grantors the property shall go to the beneficiary or beneficiaries designated in paragraph 2. Make sure you give a sufficient identification of each beneficiary. Keep in mind that you can change or revoke these designations, in writing, at any time.

In paragraph 4 fill in the name of the successor trustee. If he cannot serve, you can designate another successor trustee, or permit, as provided in paragraph 4, the first designated beneficiary to become trustee.

In paragraph 5 fill in the state of your domicile unless you wish some other state laws to govern.

The document should be fully executed by all grantors and all trustees, have two witnesses sign at the appropriate places, and have the document acknowledged. Witnesses and acknowledgment are not legally required in most trusts for personal property under most circumstances. However, it is recommended that the agreement be acknowledged and witnessed as a matter of good practice and for formality. A conveyance of real estate does require acknowledgment and witnesses. Therefore, if real estate is listed in Exhibit A you must have the agreement, and the separate real estate deed, acknowledged, witnessed, and recorded. If you have any difficulties with real estate transactions, have an attorney or a real estate expert assist in the execution and recording of the appropriate documents at the appropriate office.

In Exhibit A list in detail all property you wish to be included in the trust estate. If real estate is included it should be described with the legal description on the conveyance document (the deed or conveyance documents by which the grantor received the title to the property) and the trust agreement should be recorded along with the conveyance deeds.

You can complete the form agreements for personal property by merely listing all the property in Exhibit A. Although the execution and recording of the separate real estate conveyance documents are considered by some to be cumbersome, it is far less difficult and much less expensive than probate of the estate.

The primary purpose of the Revocation, Form 20, is to notify the trustee and to record it in the event the Revocable Living Trust Agreement was recorded. Fill in the appropriate blanks and make sure it is delivered to the trustee and recorded, if appropriate.

Form 16: Revocable Living Trust Agreement: Husband and Wife: Grantors, as Cotrustees, For Lifetime Use of Grantors, Then to Others
REVOCABLE LIVING TRUST AGREEMENT

This Revocable Living Trust Agreement is made this _(day)_ day of _(month)_, 19 _(year)_ , between _(name)_ and _(name)_ , husband and wife, of _(address)_ , City of _(city)_ , State of _(state)_ , herein referred to as Grantors, and _(name)_ and _(name)_ , of _(address)_ , City of _(city)_ , State of _(state)_ , herein referred to as cotrustees.

Whereas, grantors are now the owners of the property described in Exhibit A attached hereto and made a part hereof, and

Whereas, grantors desire to make provision for the care and management of such property, and the collection of the income therefrom, and the disposition of both such income and such property in the manner herein provided:

Now, therefore, for the reasons set forth above, and in consideration of the mutual covenants set forth herein, grantors and Trustees agree as follows:

1. *Transfer of Property:* Grantors, in consideration of the acceptance by cotrustees of the trust herein created, hereby convey, transfer, assign, and deliver to cotrustees, their successors in trust and assigns, the property described in Exhibit A attached hereto and made a part hereof, by this reference, which property, together with all other property that might from time to time be held by cotrustees hereunder, is herein referred to as Trust Estate. Grantors, and any other persons shall have the right at any time to add property acceptable to Trustees to this trust and such property,when received and accepted by Trustees, shall become a part of the trust estate.

2. *Disposition of Income and Principal:* Trustees shall care for and manage the trust estate and collect the income derived therefrom, and, after the payment of all taxes and assessments thereon and all charges incident to the management thereof, dispose of the net income therefrom and corpus thereof, as follows:

During the lifetime of grantors the Trustees might pay income of the trust estate and such portions of the principal as the grantors from time to time can direct to the grantors, or otherwise as they direct during their lives. After the death of both grantors the successor Trustee shall distribute the trust estate to the following beneficiary or beneficiaries who shall survive both grantors:

(names and addresses)

The share of any beneficiary who shall be under the age of _(age)_ years shall not be paid to such beneficiary but shall instead be held in trust to apply to his/her use all the income thereof, and also such amounts of the principal, even to the extent of all,as the Trustees deem necessary or suitable for the support,welfare, and education of such beneficiary; and when he/she attains the age of *(age)* years, to pay him/her the remaining principal, if any. If any beneficiary for whom a share is held in trust should die before having received all the principal thereof, then upon his/her death the remaining principal shall be paid to his/her then living child or children, equally if more than one, and in default thereof, to the then living descendants of the grantors, per stirpes. No interest hereunder shall be transferable or assignable by any beneficiary, or be subject during his or her life to the claims of his or her creditors. Notwithstanding anything herein to the contrary, the trusts hereunder shall terminate not later than twenty-one (21) years after the death of the last beneficiary named herein.

3. *Revocation and Amendment:* The grantors, or the survivor of them, can, by signed instrument delivered to the Trustees, revoke the trusts hereunder, in whole or in part, or amend this Agreement from time to time in any manner.

4. *Successor Trustees:* In the event of the death or incapacity of both cotrustees, we hereby nominate and appoint as successor Trustee *(name and address)* . In the event the successor Trustee does not serve we appoint whomever shall at the time be the first designated beneficiary hereunder. The trustees and their successors shall serve without bond.

5. *Trustees' Acceptance:* This trust has been accepted by trustees and will be administered in the State of *(state)* and its validity, construction, and all rights thereunder shall be governed by the law of that state.

In Witness Whereof, grantors and Trustees have executed this Agreement on the date above written.

(Signature)
Grantor

(Signature)
Grantor

(Signature)
Witness (1)

(Signature)
Witness (2)

(Signature)
Cotrustee

(Signature)
Cotrustee

Sworn to and subscribed before me this ____ day of ____, 19 ____.

My Commission Expires:
_____ *(date)*

(Signature)
Notary Public

Exhibit A

(listing of property included in this agreement)

Form 17: Revocable Living Trust Agreement: Grantor, as Trustee, For Lifetime Use of Grantor, Then to Others

REVOCABLE LIVING TRUST AGREEMENT

This Revocable Living Trust Agreement is made this _(day)_ day of _(month)_ , 19 _(year)_ , between _(name)_ of _(address)_ , City of _(city)_ , State of _(state)_ , herein referred to as Grantor, and _(name)_ , of _(address)_ , City of _(city)_ , State of _(state)_ , herein referred to as Trustee.

Whereas, grantor is now the owner of the property described in Exhibit A attached hereto and made a part hereof, and

Whereas, grantor desires to make provision for the care and management of such property, and the collection of the income therefrom, and the disposition of both such income and such property in the manner herein provided:

Now, therefore, for the reasons set forth above, and in consideration of the mutual covenants set forth herein, grantor and Trustee agree as follows:

1. *Transfer of Property:* Grantor, in consideration of the acceptance by Trustee of the trust herein created, hereby conveys, transfers, assigns, and delivers to Trustee, his/her successors in trust and assigns, the property described in Exhibit A attached hereto and made a part hereof, by this reference, which property, together with all other property that might from time to time be held by Trustee hereunder, is herein referred to as Trust Estate. Grantor, and any other persons shall have the right at any time to add property acceptable to Trustee to this trust and such property, when received and accepted by Trustee, shall become a part of the trust estate.

2. *Disposition of Income and Principal:* Trustee shall care for and manage the trust estate and collect the income derived therefrom, and, after the payment of all taxes and assessments thereon and all charges incident to the management thereof, dispose of the net income therefrom and corpus thereof, as follows:

During the lifetime of grantor the Trustee can pay income of the trust estate and such portions of the principal as the grantor from time to time can direct to the grantor, or otherwise as he/she may direct during his/her lives. After the death of the grantor the Trustee or successor Trustee shall distribute the trust estate to the following beneficiary or beneficiaries who shall survive the grantor: _____ *(names and addresses)* _____

The share of any beneficiary who shall be under the age of _(age)_ years shall not be paid to such beneficiary but shall instead be held in trust to apply to his/her use all the income thereof, and also such amounts of the principal, even to the extent of all, as the trustee deems necessary or suitable for the support, welfare, and education of such beneficiary; and when he/she attains the age of _(age)_ years, to pay him/her the remaining principal, if any. If any beneficiary for whom a share is held in trust should die before having received all the principal thereof, then upon his/her death the remaining principal shall be paid to his/her then living child or children, equally if more than one, and in default thereof, to the then living descendants of the grantor, per stirpes. No interest hereunder shall be transferrable or assignable by any beneficiary, or be subject during his or her life to the claims of his or her creditors. Notwithstanding anything herein to the contrary, the trusts hereunder shall terminate not later than twenty-one years after the death of the last beneficiary named herein.

3. *Revocation and Amendment:* The grantor can, by signed instrument delivered to the Trustee, revoke the trusts hereunder, in whole or in part, or amend this Agreement from time to time in any manner.

4. *Successor Trustees:* In the event of the death or incapacity of any Trustee, I hereby nominate and appoint as successor Trustee_*(name and address)*_. In the event the successor Trustee does not serve I appoint whomever shall at the time be the first designated beneficiary hereunder. The Trustees and their successors shall serve without bond.

5. *Trustee Acceptance:* This trust has been accepted by Trustee and will be administered in the State of _*(state)*_ and its validity, construction, and all rights thereunder shall be governed by the law of that state.

In Witness Whereof, grantor and Trustee have executed this Agreement on the date above written.

(Signature)   *(Signature)*
_____   _____
Grantor   Trustee

(Signature)   *(Signature)*
_____   _____
Witness (1)

(Signature)
_____
Witness (2)

Sworn to and subscribed before me this ____ day of ____, 19 ____.

My Commission Expires: _____   *(Signature)*
                                                                _____
(date)   Notary Public

Exhibit A

(listing of property included in this agreement)

_____
_____
_____
_____

Form 18: Revocable Living Trust Agreement: Grantor and Third Party, as Cotrustees, For Lifetime Use of Grantor, Then to Others

REVOCABLE LIVING TRUST AGREEMENT

This Revocable Living Trust Agreement is made this _(day)_ day of _(month)_ , 19 _(year)_ , between _(name)_ of _(address)_ , City of _(city)_ , State of _(state)_ herein referred to as grantor, and _(name)_ and _(name)_ , herein referred to as cotrustees.

Whereas, grantor is now the owner of the property described in Exhibit A attached hereto and made a part hereof, and

Whereas, grantor desires to make provision for the care and management of such property, the collection of the income therefrom, and the disposition of both such income and such property in the manner herein provided:

Now, therefore, for the reasons set forth above, and in consideration of the mutual covenants set forth herein, grantor and Trustees agree as follows:

1. *Transfer of Property:* Grantor, in consideration of the acceptance by Trustees of the trust herein created, hereby conveys, transfers, assigns, and delivers to Trustees, their successors in trust and assigns, the property described in Exhibit A attached hereto and made a part hereof, by this reference, which property, together with all other property that might from time to time be held by Trustees hereunder, is herein referred to as Trust Estate. Grantor, and any other persons shall have the right at any time to add property acceptable to Trustees to this trust and such property, when received and accepted by Trustees, shall become a part of the trust estate.

2. *Disposition of Income and Principal:* Trustees shall care for and manage the trust estate and collect the income derived therefrom, and, after the payment of all taxes and assessments thereon and all charges incident to the management thereof, dispose of the net income therefrom and corpus thereof, as follows:

During the lifetime of grantor the Trustees can pay income of the trust estate and such portions of the principal as the grantor from time to time can direct to the grantor, or otherwise as he/she directs during his or her lifetime. After the death of grantor the successor Trustee shall distribute the trust estate to the following beneficiary or beneficiaries who shall survive me:_____
(names and addresses)

_____

The share of any beneficiary who shall be under the age of _(age)_ years shall not be paid to such beneficiary but shall instead be held in trust to apply to his/her use all the income thereof, and also such amounts of the principal, even to the extent of all, as the Trustees deems necessary or suitable for the support, welfare, and education of such beneficiary; and when he/she attains the age of _(age)_ years, to pay him/her the remaining principal, if any. If any beneficiary for whom a share is held in trust should die before having received all the principal thereof, then upon his/her death the remaining principal shall be paid to his/her then living child or children, equally if more than one, and in default thereof, to the then living descendants of the grantor, per stirpes. No interest hereunder shall be transferrable or assignable by any beneficiary, or be subject during his or her life to the claims of his or her creditors. Notwithstanding anything herein to the contrary, the trusts hereunder shall terminate not later than twenty-one (21) years after the death of the last beneficiary named herein.

3. *Revocation and Amendment:* The grantor can, by signed instrument delivered to the Trustee, revoke the trusts hereunder, in whole or in part, or amend this Agreement from time to time in any manner.

4. *Successor Trustees:* In the event of the death or incapacity of both Trustees, I hereby nominate and appoint as successor Trustee *(name and address)*. In the event the successor Trustee does not serve I appoint whomever shall at the time be the first designated beneficiary hereunder. The Trustees and their successors shall serve without bond.

5. *Trustees' Acceptance:* This trust has been accepted by Trustees and will be administered in the State of *(state)* and its validity, construction, and all rights thereunder shall be governed by the law of that state.

In Witness Whereof, grantor and Trustees have executed this Agreement on the date above written.

(Signature) _____   *(Signature)* _____
Grantor   Cotrustee
(Signature) _____   *(Signature)* _____
Witness (1)   Cotrustee
(Signature) _____
Witness (2)

Sworn to and subscribed before me this ____ day of ____, 19 ____.

My Commission Expires: *(Signature)* _____
(date) _____   Notary Public

Exhibit A

(listing of property included in this agreement)

_____

_____
_____

_____

Form 19: Revocable Living Trust Agreement: Grantor to Third Party, as Trustee, For Lifetime Use of Grantor, Then to Others

REVOCABLE LIVING TRUST AGREEMENT

This Revocable Living Trust Agreement is made this _(day)_ day of _(month)_ , 19 _(year)_, between _(name)_ of _(address)_ , City of _(city)_ , State of _(state)_ , herein referred to as Grantor, and _(name)_ , of _(address)_ , City of _(city)_ , State of _(state)_ , herein referred to as Trustee.

Whereas, grantor is now the owner of the property described in Exhibit A attached hereto and made a part hereof, and

Whereas, grantor desires to make provision for the care and management of such property, and the collection of the income therefrom, and the disposition of both such income and such property in the manner herein provided:

Now, therefore, for the reasons set forth above, and in consideration of the mutual covenants set forth herein, grantor and Trustee agree as follows:

1. *Transfer of Property:* Grantor, in consideration of the acceptance by Trustee of the trust herein created, hereby conveys, transfers, assigns, and delivers to Trustee, his/her successors in trust and assigns, the property described in Exhibit A attached hereto and made a part hereof, by this reference, which property, together with all other property that might from time to time be held by Trustee hereunder, is herein referred to as Trust Estate. Grantor, and any other persons shall have the right at any time to add property acceptable to Trustee to this trust and such property, when received and accepted by Trustee, shall become a part of the trust estate.

2. *Disposition of Income and Principal:* Trustee shall care for and manage the trust estate and collect the income derived therefrom, and, after the payment of all taxes and assessments thereon and all charges incident to the management thereof, dispose of the net income therefrom and corpus thereof, as follows:

During the lifetime of grantor the Trustee can pay income of the trust estate and such portions of the principal as the grantor from time to time can direct to the grantor, or otherwise as he/she directs during his/her lifetime. After the death of the grantor the successor Trustee shall distribute the trust estate to the following beneficiary or beneficiaries who shall survive me: _(names and addresses)_

The share of any beneficiary who shall be under the age of _(age)_ years shall not be paid to such beneficiary but shall instead be held in trust to apply to his/her use all the income thereof, and also such amounts of the principal, even to the extent of all, as The trustee deems necessary or suitable for the support, welfare, and education of such beneficiary; and when he/she attains the age of _(age)_ years, to pay him/her the remaining principal, if any. If any beneficiary for whom a share is held in trust should die before having received all the principal thereof, then upon his/her death the remaining principal shall be paid to his/her then living child or children, equally if more than one, and in default thereof, to the then living descendants of the grantor, per stirpes. No interest hereunder shall be transferable or assignable by any beneficiary, or be subject during his or her life to the claims of his or her creditors. Notwithstanding anything herein to the contrary, the trusts hereunder shall terminate not later than twenty-one (21) years after the death of the last beneficiary named herein.

   3. *Revocation and Amendment:* The grantor can, by signed instrument delivered to the Trustee, revoke the trusts hereunder, in whole or in part, or amend this Agreement from time to time in any manner.

   4. *Successor Trustee:* In the event of the death or incapacity of the Trustee I hereby nominate and appoint as successor Trustee *(name and address)* . In the event the successor Trustee does not serve I appoint whomever shall at the time be the first designated beneficiary hereunder. The Trustee and his/her successors shall serve without bond.

   5. *Trustee Acceptance:* This trust has been accepted by Trustee and will be administered in the State of *(state)* and its validity, construction, and all rights thereunder shall be governed by the laws of that state.

   In Witness Whereof, grantor and Trustee have executed this Agreement on the date above written.

(Signature) _____   *(Signature)* _____
Grantor   Trustee

(Signature) _____
Witness (1)

(Signature) _____
Witness (2)

   Sworn to and subscribed before me this ____ day of ____, 19 ____.

My Commission Expires: *(Signature)* _____
_____   Notary Public
       (date)

Exhibit A

(listing of property included in this agreement)

_____

_____

_____

_____

Form 20: Revocable of Revocable Living Trust Agreement

REVOCATION OF
REVOCABLE LIVING TRUST AGREEMENT

TO: _____ , Trustee
                          (name)
       _____
                          (address)
       _____
                          (city, state)

    I, *(name)* , of *(address)* , City of *(city)* , State of *(state)* , as grantor in a Revocable Living Trust Agreement dated *(date)* , wherein you are designated as Trustee, do hereby revoke the powers and trusts created and conferred by grantor in that Revocable Living Trust Agreement, pursuant to the terms thereof.

    I hereby direct you, as Trustee, to turn over and deliver to me all property held by you subject to the terms and provisions of the Revocable Living Trust Agreement, together with all accumulations of interest and income.

    In Witness Whereof, I have executed this instrument on the _____ day of _____ , 19____ , at *(city, state)*.

    In the presence of:

*(Signature)*_____   *(Signature)*_____
Witness (1)   Grantor
*(Signature)*_____
Witness (2)

    Sworn to and subscribed before me this ____ day of ____, 19 ____.

My Commission Expires: *(Signature)*_____
_____   Notary Public
          (date)

Chapter 11

Other Methods of Avoiding Probate

Although the Revocable Living Trust is the classic method for avoiding probate, there are a number of other methods that you can use in your estate planning. All of them are easy to use. These plans have sometimes been referred to as *substitute wills*, in the sense that an owner of property is able to transfer it to others without having it go through the probate system by a will or statute. The use of the term *substitute will* is not literally correct, however, because probate is avoided only with respect to the specific property that is included in a probate avoidance plan; all other assets owned by a decedent would be subject to probate. Most people need a will in addition to probate avoidance plans as one does not generally wish to have all their property in a trust or other probate avoidance program. This is not to suggest that one cannot avoid probate with everything they own, but there are some general guidelines to be followed in determining who should avoid probate and for what property.

Who should avoid probate with respect to what property depends upon the particular facts and circumstances of each case. In general it is recommended that persons who are settled in their estate, family, and financial affairs should implement probate avoidance plans. Settled in their affairs is an expression that refers generally to people who own capital assets that easily can be held in trust or other probate avoidance plans; whose children are no longer minors; who have reached middle age; who have substantial assets; or who simply want to save 10% to 20% or more of an estate for their family rather than permitting it to be churned through the probate processes.

Probate Avoidance

Probate avoidance is accomplished by placing title to property in such a way that upon the death of the owner it legally passes to another who holds it outside the jurisdiction of the probate courts. In addition to the Revocable Living Trust this can be accomplished by joint ownership, joint tenancy with right of survivorship, gifts, life insurance (payable to beneficiaries other than the insured or the insured's estate), and the Irrevocable Living Trust.

Joint Ownership

The joint ownership of property with right of survivorship is one of the easiest ways to avoid probate. The jointly owned property automatically becomes that of the survivor of survivors as a matter of law and no probate is needed. The joint ownership method can be effective with real estate as well as other property, such as bank accounts, mutual funds, stocks, bonds, automobiles, and antiques. It is important for you to comply with any title certificate or recording requirements of your state. For example, automobile certificate registration or real estate conveyances must be recorded in both names as joint tenants.

Although every state authorizes joint ownership with right of survivorship, the terminology can differ from state to state. Therefore, use printed real estate forms designed for your state to convey real property titles.

In most states this method of title ownership is called *joint tenancy, with right of survivorship*. A few states call it an *estate by the entirety* when used as between husband and wife. In the eight states having community property laws, property held by husband and wife is governed by the community property principles.

Joint Tenancy, With Right Of Survivorship (JTWROS)

An estate in joint tenancy is one held by two or more persons jointly, with equal rights to share in its enjoyment during their lives, and having as its distinguishing feature the right of survivorship, or *jus accrescendi*, by virtue of which the entire estate, upon the death of a joint tenant, goes to the survivor or, in the case of more than two joint tenants, to the survivors, and so on to the last survivor, free and exempt from all charges made by the deceased cotenant or cotenants.

One of the great advantages of the doctrine of survivorship is that a joint tenant cannot devise interest in the land, for the devise does not take effect until after the death of the decedent, and the claim of the surviving tenant arises in the same instant with that of the devisee and is preferred thereto. It is equally clear that the interests of the deceased tenant cannot descend to his heirs or pass to his representatives under the laws regulating intestate succession. A surviving joint tenant holds under the conveyance or instrument by which the tenancy was created and not under laws regulating intestate succession. Furthermore, the creditors of a deceased joint tenant do not have any recourse against the surviving joint tenant who requires the property under such instrument.

At common law and also under the law as it generally prevails at present, the creation and the continued existence of a joint tenancy depends upon the coexistence of four requisites.

- The tenants must have one and the same interest.
- The interests must accrue by one and the same conveyance.
- They must commence at one and the same time.
- The property must be held by one and the same undivided possession.

In other words, there must be the following four unities: unity of interest, unity of title, unity of time, and unity of possession. If any one of these elements is lacking, the estate will not be one in joint tenancy.

In most states, these principles have been codified and are regulated by statute. When in doubt, consult the specific statutes of your own state. All natural persons can be seized or possessed of such an estate, and in most states other entities can be joint tenants.

Although most people think of joint tenancy as confined to interests in real property, it is settled that a joint tenancy of such character can exist in any kind of property. Joint ownership of bank accounts, savings accounts, brokerage accounts, and other such titles are regulated by statutes in most states, and this can easily be determined from your financial institutions. It is recommended that you discuss the subject with any financial institution where you do business to make certain that they understand, and comply with, your desires and instructions. You can't depend upon a bank, insurance company, or other financial institution to arbitrarily do your estate planning by blindly following some inter-office memo or procedure manual. They must be directed to record your accounts exactly as you specify.

You should not confuse a joint tenancy, with right of survivorship (JTWROS), with a tenancy in common. They are, legally, very different. Tenancy in common is a tenancy whereby two or more persons are entitled to land in such manner that they have an undivided possession, but several freeholds or interests. In a tenancy in common, which is not limited to husband and wife, there is no right of survivorship. Each owns undivided interests in the property. Either coowner can dispose of his undivided interest in the property during his life, or by will. When one coowner dies, his interest (an undivided interest) does not go to the surviving coowner, but to the decedent's heirs or according to will. Therefore, this kind of ownership does not avoid probate.

Tenancy by the Entirety

A tenancy by the entirety or *estate by the entirety*, exists only where the coowners are husband and wife. When either spouse dies, the survivor becomes the sole owner by right of survivorship. The right of survivorship cannot be destroyed during the lives of the coowners except with the consent of both.

In some states, this form of ownership exists only with respect to real property. In a few states it can exist in the case of personal property. For historical reasons the term estate by the entirety is still used in some states, but the legal effect is the same as the joint tenancy, with right of survivorship (JTWROS).

Community Property

Community property is property owned in common by husband and wife, each having an undivided one-half interest by reason of their marital status. The eight states with community property laws are Arizona, California, Idaho, Louisiana, Nevada, New Mexico, and Washington. The other states are governed by common law principles. Community property is that property that remains after family living expenses and all other community debts have been paid. It is said to be a fundamental postulate of the community property system that whatever is gained during coventure, by the toil, talent, or other productive faculty of either spouse, is community property. Community property, under the statutes, usually includes all property acquired by either spouse during a marriage, other than by gift, devise, or descent.

Community property is not known to the common law or to Roman law. In the United States, community property derives its existence from express legislation. It is a creature of statute and can exist only under the circumstances expressly provided for. The disposition of the property upon the death of husband or wife is governed by the statutes.

Gifts

Property you give away is no longer a part of your estate for probate purposes. Therefore you avoid probate with respect to that property. Gift taxes can be assessed, but there is an unlimited exemption for spouses, and a $10,000 exclusion annually per donee. Therefore, gifts can be used as an estate planning tool for avoiding probate and, with proper planning, for avoiding both gift and estate taxes.

Life Insurance

Generally, life insurance is payable directly to the designated beneficiaries and is not a part of an estate for probate purposes. Moreover, you can avoid estate taxes on insurance if you and your estate do not retain any ownership or interest in the insurance contract. Typically, you can have your spouse or other family member own life insurance policies on your life, and it does not become a part of your estate for probate purposes, or for tax purposes.

Irrevocable Living Trust

An irrevocable living trust, as its name indicates, is one that cannot be revoked or changed. It is final. There are some tax advantages in using an irrevocable trust, and it also has most of the advantages of a revocable trust.

This trust can be used for gifts, typically to minors. The assets in an irrevocable trust will avoid the probate system, avoid estate taxes in some circumstances, avoid income taxes to the grantor, and the trustee can manage the property for the beneficiaries if needed.

FORM 21: Irrevocable Trust Agreement

TRUST AGREEMENT

This Irrevocable Trust Agreement is made this _(day)_ day of _(month)_ , 19 _(year)_ , between _(name)_ of _(address)_ , City of _(city)_ , County of _(county)_ , State of _(state)_ , herein referred to as Grantor, and _(name)_ of _(address)_ , City of _(city)_ , County of _(county)_ , State of _(state)_ , herein referred to as Trustee.

In consideration of the mutual covenants and promises set forth herein, Grantor and Trustee agree as follows:

1. *Transfer of Trust.* Grantor herewith assigns, transfers, and conveys to Trustee the property described in Exhibit "A," attached hereto and made a part hereof by this reference, and receipt of such property is hereby acknowledged by Trustee. Such property, hereafter designated the Trust Estate, shall be held by Trustee in Trust for the uses and purposes and on the terms and conditions set forth herein.

2. *Disposition of Principal and Income.* Trustee shall administer and manage the Trust Estate, collect the income therefrom, and, after payment of all taxes and assessments thereon and all charges incident to the management thereof, apply and dispose of the net income and the principal of the Trust Estate as follows: _____ *(names and addresses of beneficiaries)* _____

3. *Additions to Trust.* Grantor and any other person shall have the right at any time to add property acceptable to Trustee to this Trust. Such property, when received and accepted by Trustee, shall become part of the Trust Estate.

4. *Irrevocability of Trust.* This trust shall be irrevocable and shall not be revoked or terminated by Grantor or any other person, nor shall it be amended or altered by Grantor or any other person.

5. *Compensation of Trustee*: The original Trustee hereunder, and all Successor Trustees, shall be entitled to reasonable compensation for their services as Trustee.

6. *Successor Trustee.* If _(name)_ (Original Trustee) resigns or is unable to continue to act as Trustee, _(name)_ (Successor Trustee), of _(address)_ , City of _(city)_, County of _(county)_ , State of _(state)_ , is hereby appointed as Successor Trustee.

7. *Governing Laws.* The validity, construction, and effect of this agreement and of the Trust created hereunder and its enforcement shall be determined by the laws of the State of _(state)_.

In Witness Whereof, Grantor and Trustee have executed this agreement on the date above written.

(Signature) _____ *(Signature)* _____
Grantor   Trustee

(Signature)
Witness (1)

(Signature)
Successor Trustee

(Signature)
Witness (2)

STATE OF _____

COUNTY OF _____   ss

The foregoing instrument was acknowledged before me this _____ day of _____, 19 _____, by _____ *(name)* _____ (Grantor), _____ *(name)* _____ (Trustee), and _____ *(name)* _____, Successor Trustee.

(Signature)
Notary Public

My Commission Expires:

_____ *(date)* _____

EXHIBIT "A"

(listing of property included in this agreement)

_____

_____

_____

_____

Part 3
Durable Power of Attorney

Chapter 12

The Power of Attorney

Estate planning is frequently thought of as what happens after death: wills, probate, avoiding probate, estate taxes, and other procedures for transfer of assets to others after death. Estate planning for what happens before death might be more important. For example, what happens in the event of disability or incompetence? This can affect you as well as other members of your family. A 22-year-old person is 7½ times more likely to suffer a disability of 90 days or more than to die. A 62-year-old person is 4¼ times more likely to suffer a disability of 90 days or more than to die. A 20-year-old person has a 79% chance of suffering a disability of 90 days or more. At age 40 the chances are 63.5%; at 60 the chances are 22%.

Have you ever thought about suffering a disability in connection with your estate plans? These statistics clearly show that although disability, unlike death, is not a certainty, it is far more likely to occur for persons under 60 than is death. The problem of disability or incompetence, therefore, requires your serious consideration in your estate plans. If you overlook this apparently remote occurrence your entire estate plans might collapse. Modern scientific methods for prolonging life has added to the likelihood of these problems.

For people who become incompetent by reason of sickness or illness, the problem of making decisions about medical care is especially troublesome. This is discussed in more detail in Part 4; however, the Durable Power of Attorney is helpful in these situations.

A power of attorney is an instrument authorizing another to act as one's agent or attorney-in-fact. It is an agency relationship between a principal and agent, and until recently was governed by common law principles of agency, which meant that an "agency" relationship was automatically terminated by the death or incompetency of the principal. Thus, under standard principles of agency law a power of attorney would be of no value if the principal should become incompetent. This untidy situation has been changed in all states during the past decade.

All states have now adopted some version of the Durable Power of Attorney Act, a model act recommended by the National Conference of Commissioners on Uniform State Laws. This statute provides that a properly executed durable power of attorney shall not terminate upon the incapacity or disability of the principal. The act provides for a statement in the power of attorney that "This power of attorney shall not be affected by subsequent disability or incapacity of the principal or lapse of time" or "This power of attorney shall become effective upon the disability or incapacity of the principal," or similar words showing the intent of the principal that the authority conferred shall be exercisable notwithstanding the principal's subsequent disability or incapacity.

It has been said that the old rule of law that a power of attorney should terminate upon incapacity or incompetency of the principal was not a very practical result. Indeed, one judge said:

> "Men who enter hospitals for major surgery often execute powers of attorney to enable others to continue their business affairs during their incapacity. Any judicial doctrine which would legally terminate such power as of the inception of the incapacity would be startling indeed—it would disrupt commercial affairs and entirely without reason or purpose."

Consider the durable power of attorney as a part of your estate plans. The forms that follow are entirely adequate for most people; however, check your own state statutes to make certain that it complies with the applicable laws of your state.

The General Power of Attorney

A power of attorney is an instrument in writing by which one person, as principal, appoints another as agent and confers upon the agent the authority to perform certain specified acts or kinds of acts on behalf of the principal. The written authorization itself is the power of attorney, and is sometimes referred to as a "letter of attorney."

The main reason for having a power of attorney is not to define the relationship as between the agent and the principal, but to evidence the authority of the agent to third parties with whom the agent deals. The person who acts under a power of attorney is called an "attorney in fact." The agent need not be an attorney at law. Any competent person can act as an attorney in fact. The term "attorney in fact" is defined by the law dictionary as:

"A private attorney authorized by another to act in his place and stead, either for some particular purpose, as to do a particular act, or for the transaction of business in general, not of a legal character. This authority is conferred by an instrument in writing, called a "letter of attorney," Black's Law Dictionary, Fifth Edition 118.

There are several kinds of power of attorney: the general power of attorney to transact business in general, the specific power of attorney that is limited to a specified act or kinds of acts, the durable power of attorney (general and specific) that expressly extends beyond the incapacity or disability of the principal.

General Principles of Agency Law

The power of attorney is essentially an agency relationship and is controlled by principles of agency law, as modified by statutes. You should not be confused by the title of "attorney in fact." An "attorney in fact" is not necessarily an attorney at law; it is merely the designation of an "agent" who is authorized to act for you. The term "agency" is a fiduciary relationship by which a party confides to another the management of some business to be transacted in the principal's name or on the account of the principal, and by which the agent assumes to do the business and render an account of it. It is a relation in which a person acts as agent for a principal pursuant to authority of the principal. The law dictionary defines "agency" as:

"The relation created by express or implied contract or by law, whereby one party delegates the transaction of some lawful business with more or less discretionary power of another, who undertakes to manage the affair and render to him an account thereof. Agency is the fiduciary relation which results from the manifestation of consent by one person to another that the other shall act on his behalf and subject to his control, and consent by the other to so act." Black's Law Dictionary, Fifth Edition 57, 58.

Who Can Make a Power of Attorney?

Any person having capacity to appoint an agent can legally appoint an attorney in fact. An insane person or a person who is incompetent is incapable of executing a valid power of attorney. This general principal of law illustrates the importance of the durable power of attorney, and the importance of making this document an essential part of your estate plans. In other words, once a person becomes incompetent it is too late to execute a power of attorney. The safe procedure is to execute the durable power of attorney so that it will be capable of covering all situations.

Form and Certainty of Instrument

In the absence of a statute, no particular form or method of execution is required for a valid power of attorney. It can be in any form as long as it shows the agent's authority, and it can be executed in accordance with any recognized common law method of executing written instruments. Since a power of attorney is ordinarily designed for use when the principal is not present, it should be executed with sufficient formality to carry on its face convincing evidence of its genuineness and in such a manner as to make it valid in law. The instrument should contain the name of the agent at the time of its execution and delivery, and the instrument must be reasonably certain and plain. A general power of attorney allows the agent to use his or her discretion as to the best manner in which to conduct the business of the principal, but a specific power of attorney that expressly designates the procedures and methods to be used must be followed by the agent.

Rules of Construction

A power of attorney must be strictly construed and strictly pursued. Under this rule of strict construction the courts generally require a specific power of attorney to articulate clearly and precisely what the agent is authorized to do. The courts will not generally extend the power to any act not expressly authorized in the document. Moreover, if the mode or method of exercising the power is prescribed in the instrument in which it is created, there must be strict compliance with those directions. However, where a general power of attorney authorizes the agent to do any act for the principal, the courts will construe the document as written and approve any and all acts reasonably within the scope of the agency relationship. In general, certain personal rights, such as voting, marrying, or writing a will, cannot be transferred to an agent.

Acknowledgment and Recording of Documents

In the absence of a statute, a power of attorney need not be acknowledged or witnessed. However, a power of attorney to convey lands or any interest in land must be acknowledged and recorded the same as a deed or mortgage. Aside from the legality of the instrument, an acknowledgment lends formality to the document. It is recommended that you use as much formality as possible in the execution of your power of attorney, and if the conveyance of real estate is involved it must be witnessed and acknowledged.

In some states the statutes require that a power of attorney for particular purposes be recorded, and these statutes must be complied with. This also relates to real estate conveyances. But in the absence of express provision of statute, the validity of a power of attorney is not affected by a failure to have the instrument recorded. In general, real estate conveyances require more formality than most other transactions. In most states acknowledgment and witnesses are required for real estate transfers, although most other transactions do not.

Duration and Revocation of Power of Attorney

The relation of principal and agent can be terminated only by the act or agreement of the parties to the agency or by operation of law. Once the relationship is established, an agency relation will be presumed to have continued, in the absence of anything to show its termination. The agreement can specify a date on which the agency shall terminate. In the absence of an agreement to terminate a power of attorney it would generally continue until terminated by operation of law. In general this means termination by death, by incapacity, acts, acquiescence or lack of acts by the parties, or other circumstances that would lead a court to declare it terminated. This rule of law illustrates the importance of the durable power of attorney in the event of incapacity.

In general a principal can terminate an agency at any time. You can usually fire your agents and employees at will. However, with a written power of attorney it is advisable to revoke the agency with the same formality as the appointment, and this requires another written instrument. It is also advisable to notify persons who have dealt with your attorney in fact that the agency is revoked or terminated.

Consent of Spouse

Most states have various laws that grant married people certain rights or interests in the assets or property owned by the married couple; these rights cannot be extinguished without the husband's or wife's consent. These rights are called community property rights, statutory rights, homestead rights, elective rights, dower, curtesy, and other names. These are discussed in more detail in Parts 1 and 2. In essence this means that a married person might not be able to legally transfer certain property owned during marriage without the written consent of the spouse. Therefore, if a married person grants a power of attorney to an agent to convey property in which the spouse has a marital interest it would be necessary to obtain the written consent of the spouse with respect to such property. This issue seldom arises in connection with a durable power of attorney because most married people usually designate their spouse as the attorney in fact, or they have the property in their joint names.

The Durable Power of Attorney

The word "durable" is defined as:

". . . lasting or enduring; holding out well against wear or any destructive change, able to continue long in the same state, having the quality of enduring, having power to resist decay, impervious to change, not easily worn out, enduring, persisting, permanent, abiding, lasting, constant, perpetual, everlasting. . .''

The term durable power of attorney is defined by the Uniform Durable Power of Attorney Act as:

". . . a power of attorney by which a principal designates another his attorney in fact in writing and the writing contains the words 'This power of attorney shall not be affected by subsequent disability or incapacity of the principal, or lapse of time,' or 'This power of attorney shall become effective upon the disability or incapacity of the principal,' or similar words showing the intent of the principal that the authority conferred shall be exercisable notwithstanding the principal's subsequent disability or incapacity, and unless it states a time of termination, notwithstanding the lapse of time since the execution of the instrument.''

This definition, based upon the uniform act, reflects the efforts of the National Conference of Commissioners of Uniform State Laws to formulate a uniform statement of the law as it should be in all states. The durable power of attorney provisions have been enacted in all states. You should have no difficulty in ascertaining the status of your state laws on this issue. A durable power of attorney is an important part of your estate planning.

The statutes vary from state to state, but most are patterned after the Uniform Durable Power of Attorney Act, which is also a part of the Uniform Probate Code. This model code is printed here to give you a better understanding of the laws. This act is not necessarily the law of any particular state, but it is a model code on which state statutes are patterned.

Statutory Provisions

The provisions of the Uniform Probate Code governing the durable power of attorney are as follows:

Section 5-501. Definition

A durable power of attorney is a power of attorney by which a principal designates another his attorney in fact in writing and the writing contains the words "This power of attorney shall not be affected by subsequent disability or incapacity of the principal, or lapse of time," or "This power of attorney shall become effective upon the disability or incapacity of the principal," or similar words showing the intent of the principal that the authority conferred shall be exercisable notwithstanding the principal's subsequent disability or incapacity, and, unless it states a time of termination, notwithstanding the lapse of time since the execution of the instrument.

Section 5-502. Durable Power of Attorney Not Affected By Lapse of Time, Disability, or Incapacity

All acts done by an attorney in fact pursuant to a durable power of attorney during any period of disability or incapacity of the principal have the same effect and inure to the benefit of and bind the principal and his successors in interest as if the principal were competent and not disabled. Unless the instrument states a time of termination, the power is exercisable notwithstanding the lapse of time since the execution of the instrument.

Section 5-503. Relation of Attorney in Fact to Court Appointed Fiduciary

If, following execution of a durable power of attorney, a court of the principal's domicile appoints a conservator, guardian of the estate, or other fiduciary charged with the management of all of the principal's property or all of his property except specified exclusions, the attorney in fact is accountable to the fiduciary as well as to the principal. The fiduciary has the same power to revoke or amend the power of attorney that the principal would have had if he were not disabled or incapacitated.

A principal may nominate, by a durable power of attorney, the conservator, guardian of his estate, or guardian of his person for consideration by the court if protective proceedings for the principal's person or estate are thereafter commenced. The court shall make its appointment in accordance with the principal's most recent nomination in a durable power of attorney except for good cause or disqualification.

Section 5-504. Power of Attorney Not Revoked Until Notice

The death of a principal who has executed a written power of attorney, durable or otherwise, does not revoke or terminate the agency as to the attorney in fact or other person, who, without actual knowledge of the death of the principal, acts in good faith under the power. Any action so taken, unless otherwise invalid or unenforceable, binds successors in interest of the principal.

The disability or incapacity of a principal who has previously executed a written power of attorney that is not a durable power does not revoke or terminate the agency as to the attorney in fact or other person, who, without actual knowledge of the disability or incapacity of the principal, acts in good faith under the power. Any action so taken, unless otherwise invalid or unenforceable, binds the principal and his successors in interest.

Section 5-505. Proof of Continuance of Durable and Other Powers of Attorney by Affidavit

As to acts undertaken in good faith reliance thereon, an affidavit executed by the attorney in fact under a power of attorney, durable or otherwise, stating that he did not have at the time of exercise of the power actual knowledge of the termination of the power by revocation or of the principal's death, disability, or incapacity is conclusive proof of the nonrevocation or nontermination of the power at that time. If the exercise of the power of attorney requires execution and delivery of any instrument that is recordable, the affidavit when authenticated for record is likewise recordable. This section does not affect any provision in a power of attorney for its termination by expiration of time or occurrence of an event other than express revocation or a change in principal's capacity.

The act defines "incapacitated person" as ". . . any person who is impaired by reason of mental illness, mental deficiency, physical illness or disability, advanced age, chronic use of drugs, chronic intoxication, or other cause (except minority) to the extent of lacking sufficient understanding or capacity to make or communicate responsible decisions." UPC, Sec. 1-201 (7).

How to Complete Your Power of Attorney

The forms at the end of this chapter are to assist you in preparing an appropriate power of attorney or durable power of attorney. Some states require that a durable power of attorney be signed with the same formality as a will, therefore, you should comply with the laws of all states where the power of attorney is to be used. A few states require recording of a durable power of attorney in some circumstances, therefore an acknowledgment provision is provided so that it can be recorded if appropriate.

The durable power of attorney, general powers, is appropriate for most people in most circumstances. It is simple and easy, and it enables you to keep your estate planning as simple as possible. If you want the power of attorney limited, execute the specific power of attorney form after specifying in the blanks exactly what you authorize your attorney in fact to do.

The durable power of attorney relating to medical treatment in "right to die" situations is discussed in Part 4.

No matter how well you plan for the probate of your estate, or plan for the advantages of avoiding probate, you will not have completed your estate planning well without addressing the serious problem of handling your estate and your personal affairs in the event of your disability or incapacity. The statistics on disability tell an awesome tale. The appointment of an attorney in fact by using the forms in this book is easy to accomplish and it has the potential for avoiding tragic consequences.

Form 22: Durable Power of Attorney—General Powers

DURABLE POWER OF ATTORNEY

STATE OF _____

COUNTY OF _____

KNOW ALL MEN BY THESE PRESENTS, THAT I, _____
_____, as Principal, of _____*(address)*_____, City of
_____, State of _____,
hereby make, constitute, and appoint _____*(name)*_____ of
_____*(address)*_____, City of _____
_____ State of _____, as my true and lawful
attorney in fact for me and in my name, place, and stead, giving unto my said
attorney in fact full power to do and perform all and every act, deed, matter,
and thing whatsoever in and about my estate, property, and affairs as fully and
effectually to all intents and purposes as I might or could do in my own proper
person, if personally present, with full power of substitution and revocation,
hereby ratifying and affirming that which my named attorney in fact shall lawfully
do or cause to be done by virtue of the power herein conferred upon him/her.
This power of attorney shall not be affected by my subsequent disability or
incapacity, or lapse of time.

_____
Witness

_____
Witness

_____
Principal

Attestation and Acknowledgment

We, _____, as Principal, and _____
and _____, the witnesses respectively, were sworn
and declared to the undersigned officer that the Principal signed the instrument
as his/her Durable Power of Attorney, that he/she signed, and that each of the
witnesses, in the presence of the Principal and in the presence of each other,
signed the instrument as witnesses, and we declare at the time of the execution
of this instrument the Principal, to our best knowledge and belief, was of sound
and disposing mind and memory and under no constraint.

_____   _____
Principal   Witness

                                           _____
                                           Witness

Sworn to and subscribed before me
this _____ day of _____, 19__. _____
                                           Notary Public

Form 23: Durable Power of Attorney—Specific Powers

DURABLE POWER OF ATTORNEY

STATE OF _____

COUNTY OF _____

KNOW ALL MEN BY THESE PRESENTS, THAT I, ____*(name)*____
_____, as Principal, of ____*(address)*____, City
of _____, State of _____
hereby make, constitute, and appoint ____*(name)*____ of
____*(address)*____, City of _____ State of
_____, as my true and lawful attorney in fact for me
and in my name, and stead, to do the following act or acts: _____
_____
_____
_____
_____

hereby ratifying and affirming that which my named attorney in fact shall lawfully
do or cause to be done by virtue of the power herein conferred upon him/her.
This power of attorney shall not be affected by my subsequent disability or
incapacity, or lapse of time.

_____   _____
Witness   Principal

_____
Witness

Attestation and Acknowledgment

We, _____, as Principal, and _____
and _____, the witnesses respectively, were sworn and
declared to the undersigned officer that the Principal signed the instrument as
his/her Durable Power of Attorney, that he/she signed, and that each of the
witnesses, in the presence of the Principal and in the presence of each other,
signed the instrument as witnesses, and we declare at the time of the execution
of this instrument the Principal, to our best knowledge and belief, was of sound
and disposing mind and memory and under no constraint.

_____   _____
Principal   Witness

                                 _____
                                 Witness

Sworn to and subscribed before me this ____ day of _____, 19____.

                                 Notary Public

Form 24: General Power of Attorney

GENERAL POWER OF ATTORNEY

STATE OF _____

COUNTY OF _____

KNOW ALL MEN BY THESE PRESENTS, THAT I, _____*(name)*_____
_____, as Principal, of _____*(address)*_____, City of
_____, State of _____, hereby
make, constitute, and appoint _____*(name)*_____ of _____
_____*(address)*_____, City of _____ State
of _____, as my true and lawful attorney in fact for me
and in my name, place, and stead, giving unto my said attorney in fact full power
to do and perform all and every act, deed, matter, and thing whatsoever in and
about my estate, property, and affairs as fully and effectually to all intents and
purposes as I might or could do in my own proper person, if personally present,
with full power of substitution and revocation, hereby ratifying and affirming that
which my named attorney in fact shall lawfully do or cause to be done by virtue
of the power herein conferred upon him/her.

_____

Witness

_____   _____

Witness   Principal

Attestation and Acknowledgment

We, _____, as Principal, and
_____ and _____, the witnesses
respectively, were sworn and declared to the undersigned officer that the
Principal signed the instrument as his/her Power of Attorney, that he/she signed,
and that each of the witnesses, in the presence of the Principal and in the presence of each other, signed the instrument as witnesses, and we declare at the
time of the execution of this instrument the Principal, to our best knowledge
and belief, was of sound and disposing mind and memory and under no constraint.

_____   _____

Principal   Witness

                                                              _____

                                                              Witness

Sworn to and subscribed before me this ____ day of _____, 19____

                                                              _____

                                                              Notary Public

Form 25: Specific Power of Attorney

SPECIFIC POWER OF ATTORNEY

STATE OF _____

COUNTY OF _____

KNOW ALL MEN BY THESE PRESENTS, THAT I, _____*(name)*_____
_____, as Principal, of _____*(address)*_____,
City of _____, State of _____, hereby
make, constitute, and appoint _____*(name)*_____, of _____*(address)*_____,
City of _____, State of _____, as my
true and lawful attorney in fact for me and in my name, place, and stead, to
do the following act or acts: _____

_____

_____

_____

hereby ratifying and affirming that which my named attorney in fact shall lawfully
do or cause to be done by virtue of the power herein conferred upon him/her.

_____

Witness

_____   _____

Witness   Principal

Attestation and Acknowledgment

We, _____, as Principal, and _____
and _____, the witnesses respectively, were sworn and
declared to the undersigned officer that the Principal signed the instrument as
his/her Power of Attorney, that he/she signed, and that each of the witnesses,
in the presence of the Principal and in the presence of each other, signed the
instrument as witnesses, and we declare at the time of the execution of this
instrument the Principal, to our best knowledge and belief, was of sound and
disposing mind and memory and under no constraint.

_____   _____

Principal   Witness

_____

Witness

Sworn to and subscribed before me this _____ day of _____, 19____

_____

Notary Public

Form 26: Power of Attorney by Corporation

POWER OF ATTORNEY

KNOW ALL MEN BY THESE PRESENTS, THAT:

_____a corporation organized
(Company)
and existing under the laws of the state of _____, and having
its principal offices at _____, City
(address)
of _____, State of _____, does hereby
constitute and appoint _____ of _____
(name)
_____, City of _____, State of
_____, its true and lawful attorney in fact for the following purposes: ____

_____

_____

_____

_____

and said company, through its board of directors, hereby ratifies and confirms
everything the said attorney in fact can lawfully do in the premises by virtue
of these presents.

In Witness Whereof, _____ has caused this instrument
to be sealed with its corporate seal, duly attesting by the signature of its this
_____ day of _____, 19____.

Name of Corporation
Address

By _____
Title of Officer

On this _____ day of _____, 19_____, before me, _____
_____ the undersigned officer, per-
sonally appeared known to me to be the person whose name he/she subscribed
to the within instrument and that he/she executed the same for the purpose
therein contained. In Witness Whereof I have hereunto set my hand and seal.

_____
Title of Officer

Form 27: Revocation of Power of Attorney

REVOCATION OF POWER OF ATTORNEY

STATE OF _____

COUNTY OF _____

KNOW ALL MEN BY THESE PRESENTS:

That, Whereas I, _____ of _____
City of , State of did on the day of , 19, by a certain instrument in writing
empower of , City of State of to act as my true and lawful attorney in fact
in my name and stead and to do and perform all matters and things pertaining
thereto as fully as I myself could do them:

Now, therefore, I *for good cause, do hereby revoke, countermand, and make
void, the power of attorney, and all powers and authority therein given and
contained, and all matters and things which shall or can be acted, done or performed by virtue or means thereof in any manner whatsoever.*

_____   _____

Principal   Witness

                                                  _____

                                                  Witness

Sworn to and subscribed before me this _____ day of _____, 19 _____.

                                                  _____

                                                  Notary Public

Form 28: Additional Specific Grants of Authority

1. *General Grant of Power.* To exercise or perform any act, power, duty, right, or obligation whatsoever that I now have or might hereinafter acquire, relating to any person, matter, transaction, or property, real or personal, tangible or intangible, now owned or hereafter acquired by me, including, without limitation, the following specifically enumerated powers. I grant to my agent full power and authority to do everything necessary in exercising any of the powers herein granted as fully as I might or could do if personally present, with full power of substitution or revocation, hereby ratifying and confirming all that my agent shall lawfully do or cause to be done by virtue of this power of attorney and the powers herein granted.

2. *Power to Acquire and Sell.* To acquire, purchase, exchange, grant options to sell, and sell and convey real or personal property, tangible or intangible, or interests therein, on such terms and conditions as my agent shall deem proper.

3. *Management Powers.* To maintain, repair, improve, invest, manage, insure, rent, lease, encumber, and in any manner deal with any real or personal property, tangible or intangible, or any interest therein, that I now own or might hereinafter acquire, in my name and for my benefit, upon such terms and conditions as my agent shall deem proper.

4. *Banking Powers.* To make, receive, and endorse checks and drafts, deposit and withdraw funds, acquire and redeem certificates of deposit, in banks, savings and loan associations and other institutions, execute or release such deeds of trust or other security agreements as might be necessary or proper in the exercise of the rights and powers herein granted.

5. *Business Interest.* To conduct or participate in any lawful business of whatever nature for me and in my name; execute partnership agreements and amendments thereto; incorporate, reorganize, merge, consolidate, recapitalize, sell, liquidate, or dissolve any business; elect or employ officers, directors and agents; carry out the provisions of any agreement for the sale of any business interest or the stock therein; and exercise stock options.

6. *Motor Vehicles.* To apply for a Certificate of Title upon, and endorse and transfer title thereto, for any automobile, truck, pickup, van, motorcycle, or other motor vehicle, and to represent in such transfer assignment that the title to said motor vehicle is free and clear of all liens and encumbrances except those specifically set forth in such transfer assignment.

7. *Tax Powers.* To prepare, sign, and file joint or separate income tax returns or declarations of estimated tax for any year or years; to prepare, sign, and file gift tax returns with respect for gifts made by me for any year or years; to consent to any gift and to utilize any gift-splitting provisions or other tax election; and to prepare, sign and file any claims for refund of any tax.

8. *Safe Deposit Boxes.* To have access at any time or times to any safe deposit box rented by me, wheresoever located, and to remove all or any part

of the contents thereof, and to surrender or relinquish said safe deposit box, and any institution in which any such safe deposit box might be located shall not incur any liability to me or my estate as a result of permitting my agent to exercise this power.

9. *Interpretation and Governing Law.* This instrument is to be construed and interpreted as a general durable power of attorney. The enumeration of specific powers herein is not intended to, nor does it, limit or restrict the general powers herein granted to my agent. This Instrument is executed and delivered in the State of _____, and laws of the State of _____ shall govern all questions as to the validity of this power and the construction of its provisions.

10. Third parties can rely upon the representation of my agents as to all matters to any power granted to my agent, and no person who might act in reliance upon the representation of my agent or the authority granted to my agent shall incur any liability to me or my estate as a result of permitting my agent to exercise any power.

To induce any third party to act hereunder, I hereby agree that any third party receiving a duly executed copy or facsimile of this instrument can act hereunder, and that revocation or termination hereof by operation of law or otherwise shall be ineffective as to such third party unless and until actual notice or knowledge of such revocation shall have been received by such third party, and I for myself and for my heirs, executors, legal representatives, and assigns, hereby agree to indemnify and hold harmless any such third party from and against any and all claims that might arise against such third party by reason of such third party having relied on the provisions of this instrument.

11. *Substitute Agent.* If _____ (name of agent) _____ ceases to act as my agent because of his death, incapacity, or resignation, I appoint _____ (name) _____ as my attorney in fact and agent.

12. *Powers of Collection and Payment.* To forgive, request demand, sue for, recover, collect, receive, hold all such sums of money, debts, dues, commercial paper, checks, drafts, accounts, deposits, legacies, bequests, devises, notes, interests, stock certificates, bonds, dividends, certificates of deposit, annuities, pension, profit sharing, retirement, social security, insurance and other contractual benefits and proceeds, all documents of title, all property, real or personal, tangible or intangible property and property rights, and demands whatsoever, liquidated or unliquidated, now or hereafter owned by, or due, owing, payable or belonging to, me or in which I have or might have hereafter acquire an interest; to have, use, and take all lawful means and equitable and legal remedies and proceedings in my name for the collection and recovery thereof, and to adjust, sell, compromise, and agree for the same, and to execute and deliver for me, on my behalf, and in my name, all endorsements, releases, receipts, or other sufficient discharges for the time.

Part 4
Living Wills

Chapter 13

Living Wills

Living wills are different from, and have little to do with, a Last Will and Testament. A Last Will and Testament, discussed in Part 1, is a written document directing what is to happen after death. A living will is a written document by a competent adult declaring that if the signer becomes terminally ill and incompetent, then life-sustaining procedures should not be used to postpone death. The purpose of the living will is to help protect the individual's right based upon the common law right to bodily integrity, the right to informed consent, and the constitutional right to privacy. This is sometimes referred to as death with dignity, or the right to die.

During the past two decades a number of significant events have evolved to make the living will an essential part of good estate planning for all Americans—young and old. Medical science has now developed the technology to sustain life almost indefinitely. Better medical care results in people living longer. In response to these developments the courts and state legislatures have adopted a series of new laws to regulate treatment—or nontreatment—of terminally ill patients. Public attitudes about death and the dying process of terminally ill patients have changed dramatically during the past few years. Finally, the costs of treatment by these extraordinary medical machines and the new medical procedures that can cost up to $20,000 per week or more, raise painful questions as to who gets treatment, who is denied treatment, who makes that decision, and who pays for it. All these events generate a plethora of profound and penetrating social, political, medical, legal, psychological, religious, ethical, and philosophical debates that will rage unchecked for a long time before it is all settled.

However, there are presently two new estate planning procedures that can answer some of these problems: the living will and the durable power of attorney.

Medical Technology

Ventilators are now used to prevent the death of thousands of patients in hospitals all over America. Dialysis machines are now used to take the place of human organs that no longer work right. Intensive Care Units (ICU's) in hospitals all over America can prolong the finality of death in almost any human body irrespective of the quality of life it produces.

Artificial body components have been added to the list of life prolonging miracles the medical research teams have perfected. Artificial hearts have not been a major success story yet, but future research will ultimately make the use of these hearts routine medical practice. Meanwhile, heart transplants and transplants of other human organs have been numerous and expensive. Artificial blood and artificial skin are now available, and no doubt the future will open the door to many other artificial body functions.

New diagnostic procedures such as computed tomographic (CT) and nuclear magnetic resonance (NMR) scanners have joined a long list of techniques used by medical professionals to diagnose patients. As the new diagnostic equipment becomes more sophisticated and the technicians who operate them become more sophisticated "experts," the patients tend to become computerized "numbers" rather than real people. Medical research has also had many success stories in the discovery of "miracle" drugs that cure or prevent many diseases and afflictions that two generations ago were the major causes of death.

As a result of these medical miracles and other improvements in medical care, the causes of death have changed dramatically. This has produced remarkable changes in the demographics in America. In 1900 the leading causes of death were influenza, pneumonia, gastritis, and tuberculosis (TB); casualties were generally young people. Today the primary threats to life are heart disease, cancer, and cardiovascular diseases; casualties are primarily older people. These causes of death attack their victims later in life and are progressive in the sense that patients often struggle for several weeks, months, or years, before succumbing. When death finally occurs, it is usually an institutional one. Frequently, dying patients spend long periods of time in a comatose or vegetative state imprisoned by an expensive assortment of medical equipment that can't awaken them, but won't let them die.

Public Attitude about Death and Dying

Two generations ago most Americans died at home in their own beds, surrounded by their families, friends, and neighbors. Doctors, who made house calls, rendered whatever medical treatments were available, and made efforts alleviate pain and discomfort for terminally ill patients. Hospital care was usually limited to extraordinary or emergency cases, and, especially during the depression years, was beyond the budget of many people. A majority of the people never reached that group of people referred today as the elderly.

Modern medicine has changed all that. Today more than 80% of the deaths occur in institutions. More than 9 out of 10 of those who die go through a long, slow decline in health from such chronic diseases as cancer, emphysema, kidney disease, diabetes, and Alzheimer's disease. Many of these patients undergo various kinds of life-prolonging treatments, such as respirators, dialysis machines, intubation, chemotherapy, and others that can virtually replace the operation of vital human organs. Most of these patients are the elderly. This array of medical machines are frequently administered to patients, many of whom are incompetent or disoriented to the extent that they cannot participate in making decisions about medical treatment or nontreatment. Frequently competent patients receive extensive medical treatment without having made a conscious decision about treatment or nontreatment. ICUs, now available in most hospitals, routinely reinflate lungs, restart hearts, fight infection, move organs from one human to another, and artificially furnish food, water, and air to those who cannot ear, drink, or breath.

Tragically, the prolonged life these extraordinary medical measures produce is low in quality, and frequently filled with pain and anguish for the patient and the family.

National polls, taken from time to time, indicate the changing attitudes of the general public about terminally ill patients. The question was asked as to whether the general public favored withholding of life support systems from terminally ill patients if that is what they want. In 1973, 62% said, yes. In 1985 the same question was answered by 82%. In 1988 affirmative responses were 91%.

While national health care for all was a big issue in the national elections of 1988, in California, a group of citizens were advocating the enactment of the California Humane and Dignified Death Act that would allow doctors to give lethal injections to the terminally ill and absolve from criminal prosecution doctors who help terminally ill patients to die. Physicians would be required to follow strict guidelines before giving the patients a lethal injection of morphine or other drugs. Under the guidelines, doctors would have to obtain a written directive from the dying patient. The directive would have to be witnessed by two nonrelatives to ensure that the patient is competent and under no duress to sign. Two doctors would have to certify that the patient is within six months of death and without hope of recovery. Opponents of the bill call it a license to kill which, if passed, would violate medical ethics and undermine the value of human life. There are strong feelings on both sides of this issue.

Euthanasia is a word derived from the Greek words *eu*, meaning well, and *thanatos*, meaning death. The word euthanasia means well or easy death or a means of inducing death or painlessly putting to death persons suffering from incurable or distressing disease. It is sometimes referred to as mercy killing.

Issues that swirl around death and dying, death with dignity, the right to die, and euthanasia generate a high degree of passion and pathos and have a wider range of views than most controversial issues. There are those who hold life very precious or simply fear death and want to remain alive as long as possible notwithstanding physical pain and agony or other ravages of terminal illnesses. There are those who want death to come quickly and quietly once they are diagnosed as incurably ill and that death is imminent. Between these two views are a wide range of opinions and ideas. Making laws to govern such transactions is not easy.

While many questions are raised by these issues, the primary purpose here is to help terminally ill, incurably ill, irreversibly ill, patients prepare, or obtain, living wills and durable powers of attorney that will reflect the patient's own views, decisions, and directives to their health care providers and family.

As the debate of these issues continue to evoke deep social, religious, philosophical, and ethical arguments, the courts and state legislatures have made some progress during the past 15 years in bringing a sense of direction to an exceedingly untidy situation. Much remains to be done in the legal and medical communities.

New Laws about Living Wills

The legal system has been slow to respond to the problems created by the right to die issues. Court cases have established some general rules, but for a terminally ill patient to be required to petition the courts for a decision about treatment or nontreatment is entirely unworkable. During the 1970s a series of court cases captured the interest of the news media and caused a public awakening of the serious health care problem presented by terminally ill patients, currently estimated to number about 10,000 at a health care cost of about one billion dollars per year.

Courts have established some legal rules and guidelines; however, many judges have strongly suggested the legal issues should be resolved by the state legislatures. Thirty-nine states had enacted living will statutes governing procedures for terminally ill patients by 1988. The other states are likely to do so soon.

In general, the state legislatures have recognized certain fundamental legal principles established by the courts. A basic premise is that all adults have a fundamental right to control the decisions relating to their own medical care, including the decision to have medical or surgical means or procedures calculated to prolong their lives provided, withheld, or withdrawn. This right is subject to certain interests of society, such as the protection of human life and the preservation of ethical standards in the medical profession. It is recognized that artificial prolongation of life for persons with a terminal condition might secure only a precarious and burdensome existence, while providing nothing medically necessary or beneficial to the patient. In order that the rights and intentions of persons with such conditions can be respected even after they are no longer able to participate actively in decisions concerning themselves, and to encourage communications between the patients, their families, and their physicians, the legislatures have declared that the living will laws shall recognize the right of an adult to make a written declaration instructing the adult's physician to provide, withhold, or withdraw life-sustaining procedures or to designate another to make treatment decisions, in the event the person is diagnosed as suffering from terminal condition.

These state statutes have a variety of different titles as shown by the list of statutes that follow, however they do have certain characteristics, including the following:

- Recognizes the right of a competent adult to making a living will regarding medical care in the event of a terminal condition.
- Gives immunity from legal liability for doctors, hospitals, and other medical caregivers who honor living wills.
- Give a sample form that might not be mandatory.
- Gives the definition of such terms as "life-sustaining procedure" and "terminal condition." The definitions vary from state to state, and you should review the laws of your own state and any state where medical treatment might be received.
- Gives procedures for execution of living wills and for witnesses, notary public, or any other requirements.
- Provides for revocation of living wills.
- Provides for making the living will a part of patient's medical files.
- Provides that a physician who is unwilling or unable to honor a living will must make a reasonable effort to transfer, or must permit the transfer, of the patient.
- Provides that nothing in the statute impairs or supersedes other rights or responsibilities any one might have to withhold or withdraw life-sustaining treatment. This clarifies that a statutory living will is now an easy way to exercise rights but that it is not the exclusive method.

The following forms are designed for use in states without living will statutes. Forms designed for use pursuant to specific state living will statutes can be obtained from:

Society for the Right to Die
250 West 57 Street
New York, NY 10107

See Part 3 for discussion of the durable power of attorney.

Form 29: Living Will

(The document that follows is the general form living will devised and distributed by the Society for the Right to Die for use in states that have not yet enacted living will legislation. The society makes available the "declaration" forms that comply with the specific statutes of each state that has enacted a living will statute. For information from this nonprofit organization and to obtain copies of any of these forms, contact the Society for the Right to Die, 250 West 57th Street, New York, New York 10107, 212-246-6973.)

Living Will Declaration

TO MY FAMILY, DOCTORS, AND ALL THOSE CONCERNED WITH MY CARE:

I, _____ (name) _____, being of sound mind, make this statement as a directive to be followed if for any reason I become unable to participate in decisions regarding my medical care.

I direct that life-sustaining procedures should be withheld or withdrawn if I have an illness, disease, or injury, or experience extreme mental deterioration, such that there is no reasonable expectation of recovering or regaining a meaningful quality of life.

These life-sustaining procedures that can be withheld or withdrawn include, but are not limited to: surgery, antibiotics, cardiac resuscitation, respiratory support, artificially administered feeding and fluids.

I further direct that treatment be limited to comfort measures only, even if they shorten my life.

(You can delete any provision above by drawing a line through it and adding your initials.)

Other personal instructions:

These directions express my legal right to refuse treatment. Therefore, I expect my family, doctors, and all those concerned with my care to regard themselves as legally and morally bound to act in accord with my wishes, and in so doing to be free from any liability for having followed my directions.

Signed _____ Date: _____
Witness _____ Witness _____

Proxy Designation Clause

(If you wish, you can use this section to designate someone to make treatment decisions if you are unable to do so. Your living will declaration will be in effect even if you have not designated a proxy.)

I authorize the following person to implement my living will declaration by accepting, refusing, and/or making decisions about treatment and hospitalization.

Name _____
Address _____

If the person I have named above is unable to act on my behalf, I authorize the following person to do so:

Name _____
Address _____

I have discussed my wishes with these persons and trust their judgment on my behalf.

Signed _____ Date _____
Witness _____ Witness _____

Form 30: Living Will Declaration:

(This is a sample form from A Matter of Choice, prepared for the U.S. Senate Special Committee on Aging)

LIVING WILL

Declaration made this _____ day of _____, 19_____

I, _____,
being of sound mind, willfully and voluntarily make known my desires that my dying shall not be artificially prolonged under the circumstances set forth below, and do declare:

If at any time I should have an incurable injury, disease, or illness certified to be a terminal condition by two (2) physicians who have personally examined me, one of whom shall be my attending physician, and the physicians have determined that my death will occur whether or not life-sustaining procedures are utilized and where the application of life-sustaining procedures would serve only to artificially prolong the dying process, I direct that such procedures be withheld or withdrawn, and that I be permitted to die naturally with only the administration of medication or the performance of any medical procedure deemed necessary to provide me with comfort, care, or to alleviate pain.

In the absence of my ability to give directions regarding the use of such life-sustaining procedures, it is my intention that this declaration shall be honored by my family and physician(s) as the final expression of my legal right to refuse medical or surgical treatment and accept the consequences from such refusal.

I understand the full import of this declaration and I am emotionally and mentally competent to make this declaration.

Signed: _____

Address: _____

I believe the declarant to be of sound mind. I did not sign the declarant's signature above for or at the direction of the declarant. I am at least 18 years of age and am not related to the declarant by blood or marriage, entitled to any portion of the estate of the declarant according to the laws of intestate succession of the State of _____ or under any will of the declarant or codicil thereto, or directly financially responsible for declarant's medical care. I am not the declarant's attending physician, an employee of the attending physician, or an employee of the health facility in which the declarant is a patient.

Witness: _____

Address: _____

Witness: _____

Address: _____

STATE OF _____

COUNTY OF _____

Before me, the undersigned authority, on this _____ day of
_____, 19____, personally appeared _____,
_____, and _____,
known to me to be the Declarant and the witnesses, respectively, whose names
are signed to the foregoing instrument, and who, in the presence of each other,
did subscribe their names to the attached Declaration (Living Will) on this date,
and the said Declarant at the time of execution of said Declaration was over
the age of eighteen (18) years and of sound mind.

[Seal]   _____

                                                    Notary Public

The Uniform Rights of the Terminally Ill Act drafted by the National
Conference of Commissioners on Uniform State Laws is printed below. This
is not necessarily the laws of any particular state, but is a model code upon which
states rely in the enactment of living will statutes. You should look to the specific
statutes of your own state and the states in which medical treatment might be
rendered.

Uniform Rights of the Terminally Ill Act (A Model Act)

Section 1. Definitions

As used in this act unless the context otherwise requires:

(1) "Attending physician" means the physician who has primary
responsibility for the treatment and care of the patient.

(2) "Declaration" means a writing executed in accordance with the
requirements of Section 2(a).

(3) "Health care provider" means a person who is licensed, certified, or
otherwise authorized by the law of this state to administer health care in the
ordinary course of business or practice of a profession.

(4) "Life-sustaining treatment" means any medical procedure or
intervention that, when administered to a qualified patient, will serve only to
prolong the process of dying.

(5) "Person" means an individual, corporation, business trust, estate, trust, partnership, association, joint venture, government, governmental subdivision or agency, or any other legal or commercial entity.

(6) "Physician" means an individual licensed to practice medicine in this state.

(7) "Qualified patient" means a patient 18 or more years of age who has executed a declaration and who has been determined by the attending physician to be in a terminal condition.

(8) "State" means a state, territory, or possession, of the United States, the District of Columbia, or the Commonwealth of Puerto Rico.

(9) "Terminal condition" means an incurable and irreversible condition that, without the administration of life-sustaining treatment, will, in the opinion of the attending physician, result in death within a relatively short time.

Section 2. Declaration Relating to Use of Life-Sustaining Treatment

(a) An individual of sound mind and 18 or more years of age can execute at any time a declaration governing the withholding or withdrawal of life-sustaining treatment. The declaration must be signed by the declarant, or another at the declarant's direction, and witnessed by two individuals.

(b) A declaration can, but need not, be in the following form:

Declaration

If I should have an incurable and irreversible condition that will cause my death within a relatively short time and I am no longer able to make decisions regarding my medical treatment, I direct my attending physician, pursuant to the Uniform Rights of the Terminally Ill Act of this State, to withhold or withdraw treatment that only prolongs the process of dying and is not necessary to my comfort or to alleviate pain.

Signed this _____ day of _____, 19 _____.

Signature _____

Address _____

The declarant voluntarily signed this writing in my presence.

Witness _____

Address _____

Witness _____

Address _____

(c) A physician or other health care provider who is furnished a copy of the declaration shall make it a part of the declarant's medical record and, if unwilling to comply with the declaration, promptly so advise the declarant.

Section 3. When Declaration Operative

A declaration becomes operative when (i) it is communicated to the attending physician and (ii) the declarant is determined by the attending physician to be in a terminal condition and no longer able to make decisions regarding administration of life-sustaining treatment. When the declaration becomes operative, the attending physician and other health care providers shall act in accordance with its provisions or comply with the transfer provisions of Section 7.

Section 4. Revocation of Declaration

(a) A declaration can be revoked at any time and in any manner by the declarant, without regard to the declarant's mental or physical condition. A revocation is effective upon communication to the attending physician or other health care provider by the declarant or a witness to the revocation.

(b) The attending physician or other health care provider shall make the revocation a part of the declarant's medical record.

Section 5. Recording Determination of Terminal Condition and Declaration

Upon determining that the declarant is in a terminal condition, the attending physician who knows of a declaration shall record the determination and the terms of the declaration in the declarant's medical record.

Section 6. Treatment of Qualified Patients

(a) A qualified patient can make decisions regarding life-sustaining treatment as long as the patient is able to do so.

(b) This act does not affect the responsibility of the attending physician or other health care provider to provide treatment, including nutrition and hydration, for a patient's comfort care or alleviation of pain.

(c) Unless the declaration otherwise provides, the declaration of a qualified patient known to the attending physician to be pregnant must not be given effect as long as it is probable that the fetus could develop to the point of live birth with continued application of life-sustaining treatment.

Section 7. Transfer of Patients

An attending physician or other health care provider who is unwilling to comply with this act shall as promptly as practicable take all reasonable steps to transfer care of the declarant to another physician or health care provider.

Section 8. Immunities

(a) In the absence of knowledge of the revocation of a declaration, a person is not subject to civil or criminal liability of discipline for unprofessional conduct for carrying out the declaration pursuant to the requirements of this act.

(b) A physician or other health care provider, whose actions under this act are in accord with reasonable medical standards, is not subject to criminal or civil liability or discipline for unprofessional conduct with respect to those actions.

Section 9. Penalties

(a) A physician or other health care provider who willfully fails to transfer in accordance with Section 7 is guilty of a class _____ misdemeanor.

(b) A physician who willfully fails to record the determination of terminal condition in accordance with Section 5 is guilty of a class _____ misdemeanor.

(c) An individual who willfully conceals, cancels, defaces, or obliterates the declaration of another without the declarant's consent or who falsifies or forges a revocation of the declaration of another is guilty of a class _____ misdemeanor.

(d) An individual who falsifies or forges the declaration of another, or willfully conceals or withholds personal knowledge of a revocation as provided in Section 4, is guilty of a class _____ misdemeanor.

(e) A person who requires or prohibits the execution of a declaration as a condition for being insured for, or receiving, health care services is guilty of a class _____ misdemeanor.

(f) A person who coerces or fraudulently induces another to execute a declaration under this act is guilty of a class _____ misdemeanor.

(g) The sanctions provided in this section do not displace any sanction applicable under other law.

Section 10. Miscellaneous Provisions

(a) Death resulting from the withholding or withdrawal of life-sustaining treatment pursuant to a declaration and in accordance with this act does not constitute, for any purpose, a suicide or homicide.

(b) The making of a declaration pursuant to Section 2 does not affect in any manner the sale, procurement, or issuance of any policy of life insurance or annuity, nor does it affect, impair, or modify the terms of an existing policy of life insurance of annuity. A policy of life insurance or annuity is not legally impaired or invalidated in any manner by the withholding or withdrawal of life-sustaining treatment from an insured qualified patient, notwithstanding any term to the contrary.

(c) A person cannot prohibit or require the execution of a declaration as a condition for being insured for, or receiving, health care services.

(d) This act creates no presumption concerning the intention of an individual who has revoked or has not executed a declaration with respect to the use, withholding, or withdrawal of life-sustaining treatment in the event of a terminal condition.

(e) This act does not affect the right of a patient to make decisions regarding use of life-sustaining treatment, so long as the patient is able to do so, or impair or supersede any right or responsibility that a person has to effect the withdrawal of medical care.

(f) This act does not require any physician or other health care provider to take any action contrary to reasonable medical standards.

(g) This act does not condone, authorize, or approve mercy killing or euthanasia.

Section 11. When Health Care Provider May Presume Validity of Declaration

In the absence of knowledge to the contrary, a physician or other health care provider can presume that a declaration complies with this act and is valid.

Section 12. Recognition of Declaration Executed in Another State

A declaration executed in another state in compliance with the law of that state or of this state is validly executed for purposes of this act.

Note: The foregoing Uniform Rights of the Terminally Ill Act is not necessarily the law of any particular state. It is a model act approved by the National Conference of Commissioners on Uniform State Laws upon which individual state statutes are patterned. The specific statutes of each state that had enacted such statutes at the time of this writing are listed in the next section.

Living Will Laws

Alabama Natural Death Act [1981], Ala. Code Sections 22-8A-1 to -10 (1984).

Alaska Rights of Terminally Ill Act [1986], Alaska Stat. Sections 18.12.010 to -.100 (Supp. 1986).

Arizona Medical Treatment Decision Act [1985], Ariz. Rev. Stat. Ann. Sections 36-3201 to -3210 (1986).

Arkansas Rights of the Terminally Ill or Permanently Unconscious Act [1987], Ark. Stat. Ann. Sections 20-17-201 to -218 (1987). [Replaces Arkansas Act of 1977.]

California Natural Death Act [1976], Cal. Health & Safety Code Sections 7185-7195 (Supp. 1987).

Colorado Medical Treatment Decision Act [1985], Colo. Rev. Stat. Sections 15-18-101 to -113 (Supp. 1986).

Connecticut Removal of Live Support System Act [1985], Conn. Gen. Stat. Sections 19a-570 to 575 (1987).

Delaware Death with Dignity Act [1982], Del. Code Ann. title 16, Sections 2501-2509 (1983).

District of Columbia Natural Death Act of 1981 [1982], D. C. Code Ann. Sections 6-2421 to -2430 (Supp. 1986).

Florida Life-Prolonging Procedure Act [1984], Fla. Stat. Ann. Sections 765.01 to -.15 (1986).

Georgia Living Wills Act [1984, 1986, 1987], Ga. Code Ann. Sections 31-32-1 to -12 (1985 & Supp. 1986), amended 1987 Ga. Laws 488.

Hawaii Medical Treatment Decisions Act [1986], Hawaii Rev. Stat. Sections 327D-1 to -17 (Supp. 1986).

Idaho Natural Death Act [1977, 1986], Idaho Code Sections 39-4501 to 4508 (1985 & Supp. 1986).

Illinois Living Will Act [1984], Ill. Ann. Stat. Chapter 110½ Sections 701-710 (Smith-Hurd Supp. 1986), as amended 1987 Ill. Pub. Act. Nos. 85-860 & 85-189.

Indiana Living Wills and Life-Prolonging Procedures Act [1985], Ind. Code Ann. Sections 16-8-11-1 to -22 (Burns Supp. 1986).

Iowa Life-Sustaining Procedures Act [1985, 1987], Iowa Code Ann. Sections 144A.1 to -.11 (West Supp. 1986), amended H.F. 360, 1987 session, 72nd Iowa General Assembly.

Kansas Natural Death Act [1979], Kan. Stat. Ann. Sections 65-28, 101 to -28, 109 (1985).

Louisiana Life-Sustaining Procedures Act [1984, 1985], La. Rev. Stat. Sections 40:1299.58.1 to -.10 (West Supp. 1987).

Maine Living Wills Act [1985], Me. Rev. Stat. Ann. title 22, Sections 2921-2931 (Supp. 1986).

Maryland Life-Sustaining Procedures Act [1985, 1986], Md. Health-General Code Ann. Sections 5-601 to -614 (Supp. 1986).

Mississippi Withdrawal of Life-Saving Mechanisms Act [1984], Miss. Code Ann. Sections 41-41-101 to 121 (Supp. 1986).

Missouri Life Support Declarations Act [1985], Mo. Ann. Stat. Sections 459.010 to -.055 (Vernon Supp. 1987).

Montana Living Will Act [1985], Mont. Code Ann. Sections 50-9-101 to -104, -111, -201, to -206 (1985).

Nevada Withholding or Withdrawal of Life-Sustaining Procedures Act [1977], Nev. Rev. Stat. Sections 449.540 to -.690 (1986).

New Hampshire Terminal Care Document Act [1985], N.H. Rev. Stat. Ann. Sections 137-H:1 to -H.16 (Supp. 1986).

New Mexico Right to Die Act [1977, 1984], N.M. Stat. Ann. Sections 24-7-1 to -11 (1986).

New York. McKinney's Public Health Law, Sections 2960 to 2978.

North Carolina Right to Natural Death Act [1977, 1979, 1981, 1983], N.C. Gen. Stat. Ann. Sections 90-320 to -322 (1985).

Oklahoma Natural Death Act [1985], Okla. Stat. Ann. title 63, Sections 3101-3111 (West Supp. 1987).

Oregon Rights with Respect to Terminal Illness Act [1977, 1983], Or. Rev. Stat. Sections 97.050 to -.090 (1985).

South Carolina Death with Dignity Act [1986], S.C. Code Ann. Sections 44-77-10 to -160 (Law. Co-op Supp. 1986).

Tennessee Right to Natural Death Act [1985], Tenn. Code Ann. Sections 32-11-101 to -110 (Supp. 1986).

Texas Natural Death Act [1977, 1979, 1983, 1985], Tex. Rev. Civ. Stat. Ann. article 4590h (Vernon Supp. 1987).

Utah Personal Choice and Living Will Act [1985], Utah Code Ann. Sections 75-2-1101 to -1118 (Supp. 1986).

Vermont Terminal Care Document Act [1982], Vt. Stat. Ann. title 18, Sections 5251-5262 and title 13, Section 1801 (Supp. 1985).

Virginia Natural Death Act [1983], Va. Code Sections 54-325.8:1 to -:13 (Supp. 1986).

Washington Natural Death Act [1979], Wash. Rev. Code Ann. Sections 70.122.010 to -.905 (Supp. 1987).

West Virginia Natural Death Act [1984], W. Va. Code Sections 16-30-1 to -10 (1985).

Wisconsin Natural Death Act [1984, 1986], Wisc. Stat. Ann. Sections 154.01 to -.15 (West Supp. 1986).

Wyoming Act [1984], Wyo. Stat. Sections 35-22-101 to -109 (Supp. 1987).

Glossary

abatement—A proportional reduction of a debt or legacy due, where the fund or the estate is insufficient to meet full payment.

acknowledgment—Formal declaration before an authorized official, by the person who executed the instrument, that it is his free act and deed.

ademption—The extinction or satisfaction of a legacy by some act of the testator, which indicates either a revocation of, or an intention to, revoke the bequest.

administration of estates—Supervision by an executor or administrator. Management of the estate by an independent executor. Normally involves the collection, management, and distribution of an estate, including the legal proceedings necessary to satisfy claims of creditors, next of kin, legatees, or other parties who might have any claim to the property of a deceased person.

administrator/administratrix—In probate practice, a person to whom letters of administration, that is, an authority to administer the estate of a deceased person, have been granted by the proper court. An administrator resembles an executor, but, being appointed by the court, and not by the deceased, he has to give security for the due administration of the estate, by entering into a bond with sureties, called an administration bond. Administrator refers to a male and administratrix to a female.

advancement—An irrevocable gift made *inter vivos* (during lifetime) by a parent to a child, with the intent that the gift is to represent all or part of the parent's estate to which the child would be entitled on the death of the parent intestate (dying without a will). An advancement is distinguished from a debt or loan in that an advancement involves a transfer of property without consideration and is also distinguished from a gift in that while the advancement need not be repaid it requires the donee to account for the gift before he or she is permitted to share in the intestate's estate.

affinity—Relation that one spouse, because of marriage, has to blood relatives of the other; consanguinity is relation by blood.

agent—A person authorized by another to act for him; one intrusted with another's business.

ancestor—One from whom a person lineally descended or might be descended; a progenitor.

ancillary administration—Administration in a state where decedent has property and which is other than where decedent was domiciled.

antenuptial—A contract made before marriage between the parties as to their property rights.

antibiotic—Any member of the group of chemical compounds produced by fungi and other microorganisms which, in diluted solution, inhibit or destroy bacteria: used in the treatment of infectious diseases, and including penicillin and the *mycin* drugs.

appraisal—A valuation or an estimation of value of property, usually by two disinterested persons of suitable qualifications.

attestation—The act of witnessing an instrument in writing at the request of the party making it, and subscribing it as a witness.

attorney-in-fact—A private attorney authorized by another to act in his place and stead, either for some particular purpose, as to do a particular act, or for the transaction of business in general, not of a legal character. This authority is conferred by an instrument in writing, called a *power of attorney.*

beneficiary—One for whose benefit a trust is created; a person having the enjoyment of property of which a trustee, executor, administrator, or other has the legal possession; a person to whom a policy of insurance is payable.

bequest—A gift of personal property.

chemotherapy—Treatment of disease by means of chemical substances or drugs.

codicil—Addition to or qualification of one's last will and testament.

collateral descent—In intestacy, this refers to descent of the intestate's heirs who are neither his descendants nor his ancestors but are those who at some point share a common ancestor with the intestate. These heirs are the intestate's collaterals. Brother or sister, uncle or aunt, nephew or niece, and so on, are all in this category.

comatose—A state of profound unconsciousness from which one cannot be aroused.

common law—The general and ordinary law of a community receiving its binding force from universal reception. Historically, that body of law and juristic theory that was originated, developed, and formulated in England.

community property—The property acquired by either spouse during marriage, other than by gift, devise, or descent based on the doctrine that property acquired during marriage belongs to the marital community. Community property states are Arizona, California, Idaho, Louisiana, Nevada, New Mexico, Texas, and Washington.

competent witness—A person who, at the time of attesting to a will, could legally testify in court to the facts to which he attests by subscribing his name to the will.

computed tomography (CT)—Computerized axial t; the gathering of anatomical information from a cross-sectional plane of the body, presented as an image generated by a computer synthesis of x-ray transmission data obtained in many different directions through the given plane.

conditional will—A will that becomes effective upon the happening of a specified condition or contingency.

consanguinity—Blood relationship; kinship; the connection or relation of persons descended from the same stock or common ancestor.

conservator—A guardian, protector, preserver. Generally appointed by a court to care for the property of another.

constructive trust—A trust by operation of law, as distinguished from an expressed trust. By construction of law, a court will establish a constructive trust in favor of one party and against another, when title is actually in the name of the latter, but when by either mistake or fraud the former has been deprived of what is rightfully his.

contemplation of death—An apprehension or expectation of approaching dissolution; not that general expectation that every mortal entertains, but the apprehension that arises from some presently existing sickness or physical condition or from some impending danger. As applied to transfers of property, the phrase *in contemplation of death* means that thought of death is the impelling cause of transfer and that motive that induces transfer is of the sort that leads to testamentary disposition and is practically equivalent to *causa mortis*. The Internal Revenue Code contains a statutory definition of the term that must be applied for tax purposes.

curtesy—Under the common law rules a husband had a right in any real property of which his wife was seized at any time during the marriage. The husband's right, termed "curtesy" was inchoate during his wife's lifetime and consummate after her death if he survived her and if a child was born of the marriage. Curtesy entitled the husband to a life estate in all of the wife's free-hold property owned by her during the marriage. It could not be defeated or by her *inter vivos* transfer or by the wife's will, and it was not subject to her debts.

decease—To die; to depart life, or from life.

decedent—A deceased person, especially one who has recently died.

descendant—One who is descended from another; a person who proceeds from the body of another, such as child, grandchild, to the remotest degree.

descent—Historically the intestate decedent's real property passed directly to his heirs by operation of law. Thus, real property was said to pass by descent to the heirs who took by inheritance.

devise—A gift of real property by will; a *devisor devises* real property to a *devisee* and the disposition is termed a *devise*.

dialysis—Literally, a separation. The act or process of separating the crystalloid elements of a body from the colloid by diffusion through a membrane.

disposing memory—One in which a person can recall the general nature, condition, and extent of property and his relations to those to whom he gives and to those from whom he withholds that property.

distribution—Historically this meant title to the intestate decedent's personal property vested in his personal representative who subsequently *distributed* it to the intestate's distributees or next of kin, after the administration of the estate which was the collection and preservation of the decedent's personal property, and the payment of his creditors.

domicile—That place where a person has his/her true fixed and permanent home and principal establishment, and to which whenever he is absent he has the intention of returning.

dower—Under the common law rules a wife had a right in any real property of which her husband was seized at any time during the marriage. The wife's right, termed *dower*, was inchoate during her husband's lifetime and consummate after his death if she survived him. The dower interest was a life estate in one-third of the real property of which the husband had been seized during the marriage. Dower could not be defeated by transfer by the husband during his lifetime or by his will, and the wife's interest was not subject to claims of his creditors. In most states this common law rule is now covered by statute and is frequently referred to as statutory share.

escheat—In American law, a reversion of property to the state in consequence of the lack of any individual competent to inherit it.

estate—This term refers to all the property owned by a decedent at his death and which passes either by his will or by the laws of intestacy. The estate for death tax purposes is not necessarily the same as for administration purposes. The value of many assets can be subject to death taxation though the assets are not subject to administration.

estate taxes—Taxes assessed by states and the federal government upon the decedent's right to transfer property. A succession, legacy, or inheritance tax is a tax upon the right to receive property.

euthanasia—The act or practice of painlessly putting to death persons suffering from incurable and distressing disease as an act of mercy.

executor/executrix—A person appointed by a testator to carry out the directions and requests in his will, and to dispose of the property according to his testamentary provisions after his decease.

fiduciary—The term is derived from the Roman law, and, as a noun, means a person holding the character of a trustee, or the trust and confidence involved in it and the scrupulous good faith and candor that it requires. A person having a duty to act primarily for the benefit of another in matters connected with the undertaking. It is something in the nature of a trust, having the characteristics of a trust, analogous to a trust, relating to or founded upon a trust of confidence.

fraud—An intentional perversion of truth for the purpose of inducing another, in reliance upon it, to part with some valuable thing belonging to him or to surrender a legal right. A false representation of a matter of fact, whether by words or by conduct, by false or misleading representations, or by concealment of that which should have been disclosed, which deceives, and is intended to deceive another so that he shall act upon it to his legal detriment.

general legacy—A legacy that is payable out of the general assets of the testator's estate, such as a gift of money, or other thing in quantity, and not in any way separated or distinguished from other things of like kind.

gift—A voluntary transfer of personal property without consideration.

gift causa mortis—A gift of personal property made in expectation of death, then imminent, on an essential condition that the property shall belong fully to the donee in case the donor dies as anticipated, leaving the donee surviving him, and the gift is not in the meantime revoked.

gift inter vivos—Gifts between the living, which are prefected and become absolute during the lifetime of the donor and the donee.

guardian—A guardian is a person lawfully invested with power, and charged with the duty, of taking care of the person and managing the property and rights of another person, who, for some peculiarity of status, or defect of age, understanding, or self-control, is considered incapable of administering his own affairs. One who legally has the care and management of the person, or the estate, or both, of a child during its minority.

guardian ad litem—A person appointed by a court to look after the interests of an infant whose property is involved in litigation.

heirs—Historically this had reference to those who took title to an intestate's real property by descent. Many state statutes now define the word to include those persons who take both real and personal property of the intestate. A living person has no heirs, but only heirs apparent.

holographic will—A testamentary instrument entirely written, dated, and signed by the testator in his own handwriting. In some states, by statute, based on the Uniform Probate Code, it is only required that the signature and material provisions of the will be in the testator's handwriting.

incompetency—Lack of ability, legal qualification, or fitness to discharge the required duty.

incurable—Of or referring to a person diseased beyond the possibility of cure.

in extremis—An extremity; in the last extremity; in the last illness.

inheritance taxes—Taxes assessed on the recipient of the assets and based on the right to receive a decedent's property.

inter vivos—Between the living; from one living person to another; gifts during one's lifetime.

intestacy—The state or condition of a person dying without having made a valid will, or without having disposed by will of a part of his property.

intestate—Without making a will. A person is said to die intestate when he dies without making a will, or dies without leaving anything to testify what his wishes were with respect to the disposal of his property after his death.

intestate laws—Statutes that provide and prescribe the devolution of estates of persons who die without disposing of their estates by law, will, or testament.

intestate succession—A succession is called intestate when the deceased has left no will, or when his will has been revoked or annulled as irregular. The heirs to whom a succession has fallen by the effects of law only are called *heirs ab intestato*.

intubation—The insertion of a tube into any canal or other part; specifically the passage of an oro- or nasotracheal tube for anesthesia or for control of pulmonary ventilation.

irrevocable—That which cannot be revoked or recalled.

legacies—Gifts of property under a will.

legatee—One who receives property under a will.

letters—This is the name given to the document issued, under court seal, to evidence to others the appointment and authority of the personal representative.

letters of administration—The instrument by which an administrator or administratrix is authorized by probate court, surrogate, or other proper office, to have the charge and administration of the goods and chattels of an intestate.

letters testamentary—The formal instrument of authority and appointment given to an executor by the proper court, upon the admission of the will to probate, empowering him to enter upon the discharge of his office as executor.

life interest—Interest held only during the term of a person's life.

lineal descent—In intestacy this refers to descent to the intestate's heirs who are his descendants, in an indefinite line of succession. For example, child, grandchild, great-grandchild, and so on.

litigation—Lawsuit; a contest in a court of justice for the purpose of enforcing a right.

living will—A written document by a competent adult declaring that if the signer becomes terminally ill and incompetent, then life-sustaining procedures should not be used to postpone death.

lunatic—A person of deranged or unsound mind, or one whose mental facilities are in the condition called *lunacy*. One who possessed reason, but through disease, grief, or other cause has lost it.

lucid interval—A temporary cure, a temporary restoration to sanity.

monomania—In medical jurisprudence, derangement of a single facility of the mind, or with regard to a particular subject, the other facilities being in regular exercise.

non compos mentis—A condition approximating total and positive incompetency. It denotes a person entirely destitute of memory and understanding.

nuncupative will—An oral declaration by the testator *in extremis*, or under circumstances considered equivalent thereto, as to the final disposition of his property, made before witnesses, and subsequently reduced to writing by someone other than the testator. Specific requirements and limitations are set out in the statutes in the states where these wills are valid.

obliteration—Erasure or blotting out of written words.

paranoia—Delusional insanity or monomania.

partial insanity—A term applied to cases wherein the mind is clouded or weakened, but is not entirely incapable of remembering, reasoning, or judging.

passage of title under a will—Title to real property passes directly to the devisee, subject to the claims of testator's creditors, but the personal representative has the right of possession during administration. Title and possession of personal property pass to the personal representative and only upon distribution of the estate does the legatee receive title and possession.

per capita—Equally, or share and share alike.

perjury—The willful assertion as to a matter of fact, opinion, belief, or knowledge, made by a witness in a judicial proceeding as part of his evidence, either upon oath or in any form allowed by law to be substituted for an oath, whether such evidence is given in open court, or in an affidavit, or otherwise, such assertion being material to the issue or point or inquiry and known to such witness to be false.

per stirpes (by the stalk)—According to the roots, or by right of representation; the issue of deceased children will take their deceased parent's share by right of representation. That mode of reckoning the rights or liabilities of descendants in which the children of any one descendant have to take only the share that their parents would have taken, if alive. For example, suppose a decedent had three children, Jim, Jane, and John, who, if living, would get one third each. If John predeceased the decedent and left ten children, the estate would be divided into twelve equal shares, if per capita. If per stirpes, the estate would be one third to Jane, one third to Jim, and the remaining one third divided among John's ten children.

posthumous child—A child born after the father's death.

pretermitted child—A child to whom a will leaves no share of the parent's estate without an affirmative provision in the will showing an intention to omit.

probate—This word describes the presenting of a will to the appropriate court to establish its validity, and the entering of the court's order finding that the instrument is decedent's will and admitting it to probate. There follows, as in intestate estates, a process of administration, the collection and preservation of the decedent's property to those entitled to it by his will or by the statute of descent and distribution.

probate court—The court that has jurisdiction with respect to wills and intestacies and sometimes guardianships. Also called surrogate's court and orphan's court in some states.

probate of will—Formal proof before the proper officer or court that the instrument offered is the last will of the decedent.

publication—The communication by the testator to the witnesses of his attention that the instrument in question should take effect as his will.

remainderman—The person who receives property remaining after the death of the person who received the original life interest.

residuary clause—The clause in a will that specifies the disposition of all that is left after indebtedness and bequests, or gifts, are paid.

residuary estate—That which remains after the debts and expenses of administration, legacies, and devises have been satisfied.

revocation of will—The recalling, annulling, or rendering inoperative of an existing will, by some subsequent act of the testator, which might be the making of a new will inconsistent with the terms of the first, or by destroying the old will, or by disposing of the property to which is related, or otherwise.

respirator—Inhaler; an appliance fitting over the mouth and nose, used for the purpose of excluding dust, smoke, or other irritants, or of otherwise altering the air before it enters the respiratory passage. An apparatus for administering artificial respiration, especially for a prolonged period, in cases of paralysis or inadequate spontaneous ventilation.

settlor—The grantor or donor in a deed of settlement. Also one who creates a trust, or furnishes the consideration for the creation of a trust.

specific legacy—A gift by will of a specific article or a particular part of the testator's estate, which is identified and distinguished from all others of the same nature, and which can be satisfied only by the delivery and receipt of the particular given thing.

spendthrift clause—A provision in a will or trust instrument that limits the right of the beneficiary to dispose of his interest and the right of his creditors to reach it.

spendthrift trust—A trust that provides a fund for the benefit of a person other than the settlor, secures it against the beneficiary's own improvidence and places it beyond his creditor's reach. Provisions against alienation of the trust fund by the voluntary act of the beneficiary or by his creditors are the usual incidents of a spendthrift trust.

statutory share—That portion of a person's property allowed to the spouse by statute.

subscribe—Literally to write underneath, as one's name (*sub,* under). To write below a documentary statement. In its popular meaning, it is usually limited to a signature at the end of a printed or written instrument.

subscribing witnesses—Those who sign as witnesses to a will.

surgery—The practice that involves the performance of operations on the human subject to cure diseases or injuries of the body.

surrogate—In American law, the name given in some of the states to the judge or judicial officer who has the administration of probate matters, guardianships, and other such matters. In other states he is called judge of probate, registrar, judge of the orphan's court, and other titles.

terminal condition—An incurable and irreversible condition that, without the administration of life-sustaining treatment, will, in the opinion of the attending physician, result in death within a relatively short time.

testamentary—The expression of an intent to dispose of property by will.

testamentary capacity—The competency to make a will.

testamentary guardian—A guardian named in the decedent's will.

testamentary power—A person who can make a will.

testamentary trust—A trust established by the terms of a will.

testate—Having made and left a valid will.

testator—A man who has left a will at his death.

testatrix—A female who has left a will at her death.

testimonium clause—The execution of a will; that clause of a will or instrument which concludes, "In Witness Whereof, I . . .''

testimony—Evidence given by a competent witness, under oath or affirmation, as distinguished from evidence derived from writing and other sources.

trust—In general, a right of property, real or personal, held by one party for the benefit of another.

trustee—One to whom property or funds have been legally entrusted to be administered for the benefit of another; a person, usually one of the persons appointed to administer the affairs of a company, institution, or the like.

trustor—One who creates a trust. Also called a settlor or grantor.

valid—Sufficiently supported by actual fact, well grounded, sound, or just; good or effective, having sufficient legal strength or force; good or sufficient in point of law.

validity—The state or quality of being valid; legal strength or force; soundness.

void—Having no legal or binding force; null. Empty or not containing matter, vacant, unoccupied, devoid, destitute.

will—An instrument executed by a competent person in the manner prescribed by statute, whereby he makes a disposition of his property to take effect on and after his death.

Index

Index

Other Bestsellers From TAB

☐ **INSTANT LEGAL FORMS: Ready-to-Use Documents for Almost Any Occasion—Ralph E. Troisi**

By following the clear instructions provided in this book, you can write your own will, lend or borrow money or personal property, buy or sell a car, rent out a house or apartment, check your credit, hire contractors, and grant power of attorney—all without the expense or complication of a lawyer. Author-attorney Ralph E. Troisi supplies ready-to-use forms and step-by-step guidance in filling them out and modifying them to meet your specific needs. 224 pp., illustrated.
Paper $11.95   Hard $15.95
Book No. 30028

☐ **FIGHT THE IRS AND WIN! A Self-Defense Guide for Taxpayers—Cliff Roberson**

With this practical guide you can obtain the best results possible—protect your individual and property rights—in any dispute with the IRS. The outstanding feature of this book is that it takes complicated IRS operations and provides the average taxpayer with advice on how to protect himself in IRS controversies. It is the taxpayer's self-defense book. 224 pp.
Paper $19.95   Hard $24.95
Book No. 30021

☐ **RETIRE IN STYLE—The Lifetime Security Planning Guide—Edward S. Soltesz**

Here is a comprehensive guide to retirement planning that can help ensure financial security for your golden years. Soltesz shows you how to build a secure retirement nest egg. Step-by-step guidance, examples, and worksheets are supplied for planning your successful retirement. Specific advice for people already retired is also presented. 300 pp.
Paper $12.95   Hard $15.95
Book No. 30017

☐ **GOING PUBLIC: How to Make Your Initial Stock Offering Successful—Martin Weiss**

This book contains the essential information business owners need to prepare for the problems, pressures and dangers of offering public stock. *Going Public* is a concise and extremely well-written overview of the process. Using the businessman's perspective, this guide covers: factors that affect the stock offering, finding a proficient undersriter, pricing the stock, dilution of earnings, and more. 168 pp., 47 illus., 6″ × 9″.
Hard $19.95   Book 30012

☐ **THE 10% SOLUTION: Your Key to Financial Security—Ed Blitz**

A foolproof method for lifelong financial planning! Blitz shows how you can build a small fortune, simply by saving consistently. If you can put away just 10% (or 5%, or 2%) of all the money you receive—whether earnings, gifts, or dividends—you will soon have a substantial sum of money saved. Blitz explains how to stick to this simple plan, and addresses the opportunities for investing and tax planning that increasing wealth will bring. 200 pp.
Paper $10.95   Hard $12.95
Book No. 30023

☐ **UNDERSTANDING WALL STREET—2nd Edition—Jeffery B. Little and Lucien Rhodes**

"An excellent introduction to stock market intracacies" —**American Library Association Booklist**

This bestselling guide to understanding and investing on Wall Street has been completely updated to reflect the most current developments in the stock market. The substantial growth of mutual funds, the emergence of index options, the sweeping new tax bill, and how to keep making money after the market reaches record highs and lows are a few of the things explained in this long awaited revision. 240 pp., 18 illus., 6″ × 9″.
Paper $14.95   Hard $19.95
Book No. 30020

☐ **THE NEW—IDEA SUCCESS BOOK: Starting a Money-Making Business—Al Riolo and Ellen Greenberg**

Join the entrepreneurial revolution! Small business is "big business" these days, and you can be a part of the boom! This book is designed to take you from inspiration to pay-off, step by step. Detailed guidance is provided in: choosing a business idea. A financing, setting up your business, marketing,and making the U.S. Government an ally. 220 pp., Illustrated.
Paper $10.95   Hard $12.95
Book No. 30013

☐ **EVERYDAY LAW FOR EVERYONE—John C. Howell**

By following this guide you will be able to: write your own will, change your name, win landlord/tenant disputes, set up partnerships, avoid probate, adopt a child, form your own corporation, and draw up business contracts, and more—without the expense or complications of hiring a lawyer! 238 pp.
Paper $9.95   Book No. 30011

Other Bestsellers From TAB